FAT BROKE & CRAZY

Rediscovering the Fruit of **SELF-CONTROL**

J. CHRISTOPHER McMICHAEL

Fat, Broke, and Crazy:
Rediscovering the Lost Fruit of Self-Control
Copyright © 2019 by J. Christopher McMichael
Second Printing

Published by Engrafted Word Church
5 W. Broad Street, Cookeville, TN 38501
www.EngraftedWord.org

All rights reserved. No part of this book may be reproduced or transmitted in any form or by any means without written permission from the author.

ISBN: 978-1-7339629-0-2

Unless otherwise indicated, all Scripture quotations are from the King James Version of the Bible.

Scripture quotations labeled NASB are from the New American Standard Bible® (NASB), Copyright © 1960, 1962, 1963, 1968, 1971, 1972, 1973, 1975, 1977, 1995 by The Lockman Foundation. Used by permission.

Scripture quotations marked NIV are taken from the Holy Bible, New International Version®, NIV®. Copyright © 1973, 1978, 1984, 2011 by Biblica, Inc.™ Used by permission of Zondervan. All rights reserved worldwide. www.zondervan.com. The "NIV" and "New International Version" are trademarks registered in the United States Patent and Trademark Office by Biblica, Inc.™

Scripture quotations marked NLT are taken from the Holy Bible, New Living Translation, Copyright © 1996, 2004, 2015 by Tyndale House Foundation. Used by permission of Tyndale House Publishers, Inc., Carol Stream, Illinois 60188. All rights reserved.

Quotations designated NET are from the NET Bible® copyright ©1996, 2019 by Biblical Studies Press, L.L.C. http://netbible.com All rights reserved.

Scripture quotations marked CSB have been taken from the Christian Standard Bible®, Copyright © 2017 by Holman Bible Publishers. Used by permission. Christian Standard Bible® and CSB® are federally registered trademarks of Holman Bible Publishers.

Cover layout by Darrell Kerley
Printed in the United States of America

Dedication

To the American Church. May she return to her first love in strength, discipline, and power.

Table of Contents

Introduction 1

Chapter 1 The Fruit of the Spirit 5

Chapter 2 The Need for a Cultural Overhaul 21

Chapter 3 Self-Control in the New Testament 33

Chapter 4 On the Nature of Self-Control 51

Chapter 5 Soul Discipline 71

Chapter 6 Financial Discipline 97

Chapter 7 Appetite Discipline 135

Chapter 8 Final Thoughts 159

INTRODUCTION

As a pastor, I take my assignment from God very seriously. I am ever mindful that one day I will stand before God and give an account for the job I did as a local shepherd over His flock. I understand that I will be judged according to both the quality of my pastoring and the attitude with which I did it. As a pastor, I understand that I am to spiritually feed, water, protect, and comfort my flock. I don't exist to entertain God's people. I am called to perfect them.

In pastoring, I am always watching my congregation (and the Body of Christ in general) to see what need currently requires attention. Part of the pastor's duty is to aid the flock where it is weakest. Good pastors have learned to triage flock issues and address them accordingly. I have learned that the best way to strengthen any weakness in my church is to teach a series of lessons or sermons addressing that particular weakness and prescribing God's solution.

I have also observed that the quality of the sheep under my pastorate is a result of my pastoring. Weak sheep are the result of weak pastoring. Dirty sheep are the result of dirty pastoring. Strong sheep are the result of strong pastoring. In essence, my sheep are a reflection of my pastorate, and my church's reputation is an extension of my own.

Pastoring in the Southeastern United States (also called *the South*) requires that I address certain cultural sins and weaknesses on a regular basis. I have often joked (and it's only humorous if you understand Southern culture) that the South excels at three things: obesity, poverty, and college football. This stereotype is not without merit.

At the time of this publication, 7 out of the 10 fattest states in America are in the South.[1] (Coincidently, all seven of these obese states also have really good college football programs.) Southern states also have 8 of the top 10 highest poverty rates in America.[2] But . . . Southeastern colleges

---

[1] Mississippi (1), Alabama (3), Louisiana (4), South Carolina (5), Tennessee (6), Kentucky (7), and Arkansas (9). According to the CDC.

[2] Mississippi (50), Louisiana (48), Alabama (47) Kentucky (46), Arkansas (45), Georgia (44), West Virginia (43), Tennessee (41), South Carolina (40).

have won 17 of the last 20 NCAA College Football Championships. All of that to say, I know the culture of the region where I pastor.

In addressing the poverty of my region and the obesity of my own church, I have spent years regularly teaching on the spiritual fruit of self-control. Though I have often felt like a broken record teaching the same truths over and over again, the Bible encourages the weary preacher to persevere, because faith comes by hearing and hearing. I have discovered you can have what you preach, and preaching self-control produces self-control. And the good news is self-control works! Our church no longer resembles the statistics of the South. We have prospered. We have lost a lot of weight. We are healthier and more productive as a local church body. I can testify that the fruit of self-control can fix almost any self-inflicted problem—it just has to be taught.

In 2016, in one week's time, I ran across three separate news headlines. The first read something to the effect: *Thirty Percent of Americans Obese*. The next read: *One-third of Americans Don't Have One Dollar in Savings*. And the last article read: *One in Four Americans Mentally Ill*. My heart sank. Here, in three succinct headlines, was the testimony of my nation, America—the Christian Nation. One-third obese. One-third broke. One-third mentally ill.[3] I instantly had several thoughts: "The Bible deals with each of these areas. A lot." "These problems are so easily addressed by self-control." "How many of these 'thirds' overlap?" (see fig. 1) "How many of these 'thirds' are born-again believers?" and "What is going on with the Body of Christ?"

These statistics, these "thirds," stand in stark contrast to America's worldwide reputation. America is known for having the world's most advanced medical technology. She is known as the wealthiest nation in human history. And America is known for having the greatest universities and for being the most educated population ever. Yet our national statistics declare we are one-third fat, one-third broke, and one-third mentally ill. Thus, the inspiration for this book's title—*Fat, Broke, & Crazy*.

---

[3] For practical purposes, I have taken the liberty to round up the mental illness statistics from 25% to 33%. Time will eventually do so anyway.

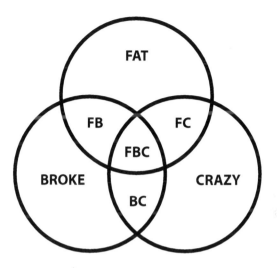

Figure 1—A classic Venn Diagram. FB—Fat and Broke; FC—Fat and Crazy; BC—Broke and Crazy; FBC—Fat, Broke, and Crazy.

But what is going on and what can be done? It may be an oversimplification, but the answer is: the end of all things is at hand. The fruit of lawlessness and sinful indulgence is being harvested. Generations of poor parenting are coming home to roost. Decades of slowly drifting away from God's Word and the practice of God's Word are beginning to catch up with us as a nation. The Bible simply calls it "the bondage of corruption."[4] The solution, at least for the Christian, is to get back to doing the Bible.

For the Christian, the Bible is our answer book. It offers us the wisdom of God for any and every type of problem we may face. This includes obesity, poverty, and mental illness. It is at this point that I must clearly state I am neither a dietician nor a medical doctor. I am neither an accountant nor a financial planner, nor am I a psychologist or psychiatrist. I do not purport to offer professional advice or direction in contradiction to professionals in these three arenas. What I am is a pastor and Bible teacher. What I do purpose to offer with this book is an exposition of the Scriptures and Bible doctrines that apply to these three areas of life. I believe if you'll mix the supernatural wisdom of God's

---

[4] Romans 8:21

Word with the natural wisdom of secular professionals, your situation can turn very quickly for the better. The purpose of this book is to build a faith that will birth a changed lifestyle.

This book has been written with the American Church as the target audience. No doubt, it contains universal truths that will help any believer in the Christian walk, but it also contains a lot of American cultural references and colloquialisms. If you can get past the candid title—*Fat, Broke, & Crazy*—this book will offer you a wealth of knowledge, hope, and biblical truth. But do realize, simply reading this book won't make you skinny, rich, or sane. On the contrary, reading this book will simply give you the biblical knowledge you need to turn these areas around. If you're reading this and recognize that you fall under one of these three categories—overweight, financially hurting, or struggling with mental instability—do not be discouraged. Though things will not change overnight, they will begin to change if you will do the Word of God and apply the fruit of self-control!

J. Christopher McMichael

CHAPTER 1
THE FRUIT OF THE SPIRIT

Jesus made a powerful statement in John 16:7, saying, "But I tell you the truth, it is to your advantage that I go away; for if I do not go away, the Helper will not come to you; but if I go, I will send Him to you" (NASB). The departure of Jesus Christ after His resurrection was necessary for the Church to receive the Holy Spirit and all of His supernatural help. Much has been said and written about the New Testament ministry of the Holy Spirit, so I will only briefly summarize it here.

Jesus called the Holy Spirit the Spirit of Truth. He is our Helper, our Comforter, our Guide, and the Revealer of things to come. He is the third person of the Godhead and He is God. In fact, He is the first person of the Godhead to be revealed in the Bible.[1] To be ashamed of the Holy Spirit's presence in our lives or even in our church services is to be ashamed of God Almighty.

There are nine supernatural manifestations ascribed to the Holy Spirit's ministry, commonly called the Gifts of the Spirit. The Gifts of the Spirit are called *manifestations* in 1 Corinthians 12:7 because they describe how He manifests through the individual believer in order to profit mankind. The original Greek definition for manifestation includes the term *exhibition.* When one attends a martial arts exhibition, they are guaranteed to see a martial artist show off what he or she is capable of. In like fashion, these nine[2] "gifts" are how the Holy Spirit *exhibits,* or shows off His power, in and through the Body of Christ. I think it might really help our services if we went to church expecting a Holy Spirit exhibition.

---

[1] See Genesis 1:2.
[2] According to 1 Corinthians 12:8-10 the nine Gifts of the Spirit are: the word of wisdom, the word of knowledge, special faith, gifts of healing, working of miracles, prophecy, discerning of spirits, divers kinds of tongues, and interpretation of tongues. For a thorough study on the subject, see the Pentecostal classic *Questions & Answers On Spiritual Gifts* by Howard Carter. Oklahoma: Harrison House, 1976.

After all, He is known for confirming the Word with signs following.³

Not surprisingly, these nine gifts are favored by Pentecostals and loathed by Cessationists.⁴ But as wonderful and necessary as the Gifts of the Spirit are, it must not be forgotten that the believer does not and cannot control the manifestation or exhibition of the Holy Spirit. The Holy Spirit manifests and shows off as *He*, God, wills (remember, the Holy Spirit is God),⁵ not as we will. This makes the Gifts of the Spirit a type of micro-sovereign move of God that even the most ardent Pentecostal can only yield to at best. Alas, we cannot "turn on" the Gifts of the Spirit, neither can we turn them "off." We can only covet earnestly after them, forbidding not to speak with tongues, despising not prophecy, yielding to the other gifts as He manifests, and then do our best to never grieve, quench, or frustrate the Spirit of Grace as He seeks to use us to bless others.⁶

In contrast, the Fruit of the Spirit are in many ways just the opposite in nature to the Gifts of the Spirit. Whereas the Gifts of the Spirit are spontaneous, turning off just as quickly as they turn on, and being totally out of the control of the individual believer, the Fruit of the Spirit take time to develop. They must be cultivated and are the total responsibility of the individual Christian. The Fruit of the Spirit must be developed through Bible study, prayer, and application. Like natural fruit, with time and the proper conditions, the Fruit of the Spirit can and should grow

---

³ Mark 16:20

⁴ Cessationism is a doctrine stating that the nine Gifts of the Spirit (and the miraculous power of God) have ceased and are no longer available to the Church today. The point in time when the gifts are said to have passed away varies. Some hold that they passed away with the last Apostle; others hold to the date of 70 AD corresponding to the destruction of the Temple in Jerusalem; some believe the miraculous ceased once the last epistle of the New Testament was written, about 96 AD; still others believe the supernatural ceased once we had the codified Bible. However, the Bible as we know it was nowhere close to being codified before the 4th Century. Lists of God-breathed books were being suggested at this time; specifically, Athanasius' Easter letter from 367 AD, the Council of Rome in 382 AD, and then finally the Council of Hippo in 393 AD. The inspiration of The Revelation was also being debated for many more hundreds of years after the 4th Century. I would think a doctrine this critical should be able to be nailed down with a little more accuracy than, say, a 1,000 year window of time.

⁵ 1 Corinthians 12:11

⁶ See 1 Corinthians 12:31; 14:39b; 1 Thessalonians 5:20; Ephesians 4:30; 1 Thessalonians 5:19; and Galatians 2:21, respectively.

larger in our lives. For example, the fruit of "little patience" today, should with time and application grow into the fruit of "longsuffering."

It is very easy to be infatuated with the Gifts of the Spirit while neglecting the Fruit of the Spirit. To be sure, we need both! The gifts "profit withal" and show off the power of God, but the Fruit of the Spirit prove we have "crucified the flesh with its affections and lusts"[7] and that we are abiding in Him.[8] It must also be kept in mind that it is possible to have the gifts without manifesting the fruit (see Balaam, Eli, and Judas). It is also possible to have the gifts without being a true disciple of Jesus Christ, for many will say to Him in that day, "Lord, Lord, have we not prophesied in thy name? And in thy name have cast out devils? And in thy name done many wonderful works [miracles]?"[9]

Clearly, the Gifts of the Spirit don't impress Jesus. But we must not forget something else Jesus Christ emphasized, "My Father is glorified by this, that you bear much fruit, and so prove to be My disciples."[10] The Fruit of the Spirit growing and manifesting in our lives not only glorifies the Father, they also prove we are *true* disciples of Jesus Christ. We are known by our fruit. Proverbs 20:11 states, "Even a child is known by his doings, whether his work be pure, and whether it be right."

Spiritual Gifts Don't Prove Maturity

Some Pentecostal Christians erroneously equate *spirituality* with *Christian maturity*. And since Pentecostals love the Gifts of the Spirit, then anyone who is used in the Gifts of the Spirit is deemed "spiritual." If someone has a dream or a vision, they are often regarded as spiritual. The church "prophetess" is often esteemed as spiritual because she always seems to have a "word" for everyone in the congregation. The worship leader may sing in the Spirit and therefore be counted as spiritual. It seems the unspoken rule of Pentecostals is: *He that is most publicly used by God must be the most spiritual.* There may be a partial truth to this, for being used by the Spirit of God can involve you in

---

[7] Galatians 5:24
[8] John 15:4
[9] Matthew 7:22
[10] John 15:8 (NASB)

spiritual things, but we may want to consider readjusting our lingo and our metrics. I believe my point will become clear as we proceed.

We should ask some probing questions. Is "spiritual" the same as "mature"? Is "spiritual" the same as "fruitful"? Are we simply looking for spiritual people? Shouldn't we be looking for mature Christians? Witches are spiritual, but we would never call them mature or fruitful Christians. Likewise, psychics are spiritual, but we would never confuse their works as Christ-honoring fruit. Balaam was spiritual but greedy. Eli was spiritual but obese and partial in judgment. Judas was spiritual but also greedy and traitorous. The Spirit of God used these men in supernatural ways, e.g., visions, revelations, prophecies, healing the sick, casting out devils, even preaching the Gospel, but these men all died horrific, unnatural deaths like pagans. They can hardly be described as mature.

Balaam, Eli, And Judas

On the outside these three men had impressive public testimonies. There's Balaam the prophet bragging about how often he talks to Jehovah and how often Jehovah talks back to him; how angels appear to him and even appear to his own donkey (that man's _so_ spiritual, even his donkey sees angels); how he turned down great wealth in order to obey Jehovah and bless a group of nomadic former slaves (what a social justice warrior); how he was once in the Spirit and God showed him a Star coming out of Jacob and a Scepter rising out of Israel;[11] and how he could not but obey the anointing of God on his life even if it meant angering a foreign king. What a prophet!

And we have Eli the high priest, explaining how he daily sees the glory of God in the tabernacle at Shiloh; how proud he is of his sons who serve in the ministry too; how he's not afraid to confront sin in the people, especially public intoxication; how he has prophesied babies and the barren conceive; how he once trained up a boy whose existence was the result of one of his own prophecies; how even though his eyesight is failing he still knows the voice of God; how he's faithful to care for the Ark of God. What a high priest!

---

[11] Numbers 24:17

And there's Judas, one of the twelve. Hear how he testifies of his public ministry; how he has walked with the Lord for over three years; how he spends hours praying with the Lord; how he's helped distribute supernaturally multiplied fishes and loaves, not once but twice; how he's commissioned to go out and preach the Gospel; how he's healed the sick, cast out devils, and raised the dead; how he judged a few cities and dusted his feet off at them; how he's even the Lord's personal treasurer. What a disciple!

But what of their private lives? Because these all died leaving no fruit that remained.[12]

Balaam was a soothsayer, sometimes speaking for God, sometimes channeling familiar spirits. He was a prophet-for-hire having learned how to merchandise his gifting. He was stubborn in his greediness and repeatedly disobeyed God in private. His donkey was more submissive than he was and actually saw the angel first. Publicly, he appeared to be the premier prophet of his day, being sought out by kings and sultans, but privately he was a greedy conniver who betrayed Israel. The New Testament remembers him as the "mad prophet."[13] He died a brutal death among those who paid him his last paycheck. Publicly, he appeared to be spiritual, but privately he was nothing but a greedy soothsayer. Balaam can hardly be remembered as mature or praiseworthy.

What about Eli, high priest and second-to-last judge of Israel? What was his true testimony? Eli was obese having spent years gorging himself on the chiefest of the Lord's offerings. He was the original ministry fat cat—literally. His sons were sons of Belial (what the NASB calls "worthless fellows") guilty of embezzling the tithe and sleeping with the tabernacle handmaidens. Even worse, Eli never restrained his sons nor removed them from office, even honoring them above Jehovah God. When an unnamed man of God ultimately declared his judgment,[14] Eli showed no remorse nor demonstrated any attempt at repentance. The last day of his life, his sons died in battle and the Ark of God was stolen.

---

[12] John 15:16

[13] See 2 Peter 2:16. The irony of this story is that the donkey, the most stubborn of all animals, has a personal testimony of total submission and faithfulness to Balaam. The donkey is used of God to rebuke the stubbornness of the prophet.

[14] See 1 Samuel 2:27-36.

The news of these horrific events caused the old priest to fall backwards off his chair, breaking his neck under his tremendous weight. Publicly, he appeared spiritual, but privately he was a compromised slob that had been rejected and despised by God. Eli can hardly be remembered as mature or praiseworthy.

And what about Judas? He was a thief from the beginning. He cared nothing for the people, only their possessions. When Mary anointed the Lord's feet with the costly spikenard, Judas was not moved by the demonstration of love and sacrifice; he wanted to know why it was being wasted on Jesus and not sold for almsgiving. He did not see the ministry in terms of souls hurt and souls helped, but he saw everything in terms of money. He eventually sold his soul, and then he sold the Lord. All that money ever bought anybody was a field of blood.

Publicly, Judas was indistinguishable from the other disciples. Even they were deceived by Judas' false public piety. When the Lord declared, "one of you shall betray me," eleven voices asked "Lord, is it I?" not "It's going to be Judas, duh!" No one suspected Judas. He was *that* convincing. The New Testament remembers him as "the traitor" and "the son of perdition." He hanged himself, went to hell, and was quickly replaced by Matthias. Publicly, he appeared spiritual, but privately he was a devil. Judas can hardly be remembered as mature or praiseworthy.

It is time we revisit what the Bible defines as mature and praiseworthy.

Honoring The Profane

How did we drift into such a place, where we fail to recognize what God calls mature while idolizing what He calls profane? It should not shock any reader that American culture is saturated and inundated with entertainment. Our entire modern culture has been driven, shaped, and defined by spectatorship. Americans are easily star-struck. Our culture has conditioned us to congregate in a collection of seats, all face the same direction, and await the voice of entertainment. He or she who stands to entertain those in the seats is generally regarded as the greatest of them all. We do this at concerts, movie theaters, stage plays, political events, graduations, dance recitals, comedy clubs, and even classrooms. I suppose this mindset is fine for the purpose of entertainment, but it proves catastrophic when it's brought into the Church.

When God's people walk into a church, having been conditioned by Western entertainment habits, they find seats arranged toward a platform and pulpit just like at a venue for entertainment. And unless they are taught otherwise, their hearts cannot help but assume an internal posture prepared to consume entertainment and idolize the entertainer. You can understand why many Westerners view church as "Sunday morning entertainment." This may help to explain why so few Christians want to contribute any time, talents, or sacrifice to the House of God—after all, such things are not required anywhere else in the entertainment world. Some churches have even played into this trap, no longer calling their church services "services." They have mixed the sacred with the secular and call their Sunday services "worship *experiences.*" *T-minus 2 days, 11 hours, 13 minutes until the next worship experience* reads the church website ticker—as if the church members were in line at Disney.

With this understanding in mind, consider now how it will look to the nominal, mediocre, lukewarm, Sunday-morning-only Christian, when someone gets up to sing, preach, or even prophesy. He or she who sings the loudest, preaches the strongest, or prophesies the most divine cannot help but be considered *the greatest showman.* They are standing in the limelight and therefore are greater than those seated. These people are "upfront" and therefore they must be spiritual, right? They are "onstage" and therefore must be mature, right? They have the microphone and therefore must be the most qualified, right? They must have it all together like all the other famous people do, right? Unfortunately, sometimes this couldn't be further from the truth.

What the average congregational member is observing on Sunday morning is a demonstration of public ministry, not private character. Public ministry is what you do in front of the congregation. Private character is defined by how you privately walk with God. As should be expected, public ministry is not always the best indicator of private character.[15]

---

[15] My previous book *Samson: Secrets to Destroying Your Life and Ministry* covers this subject in depth.

What the congregation fails to see is the minister's private application of Scripture. The average Christian mistakes public ministry for spiritual fruit. Why? Because our culture is drunk with celebrity worship and showmanship. I humbly present that, unfortunately, the Gifts of the Spirit and many other Kingdom giftings (singing, public speaking, exhortation, etc.) lend themselves all too easily to the pride of showmanship. Praise and worship time is no longer about honoring the presence of God; it has become a concert, or worse yet, just a stepping-stone toward some reality-TV song show. The pulpit ministry is no longer about preaching the Word of Righteousness, teaching sound doctrine, or perfecting the saints; it has become a platform for motivational feel-goodism and pop-culture prattling. The true gift of exhortation whereby God's people are encouraged, recharged, and fired-up has become muddied with cheap rhyming schemes, sing-song hack gimmicks, and carefully produced mantras that cue the congregation when it's time to "get wild."

These Sunday performers are on display, not in front of an unchurched secular audience ignorant to modern church culture, but an audience that can appreciate and esteem them. This is church, therefore those who are upfront and seen are often labeled "spiritual" and "mature." But what if the private lives of those platform ministers were really defined by rudeness, hatefulness, revolving debt, obesity, pride, an undisciplined mind, a dysfunctional marriage, sexual sin, or constant irritation and vexation of soul? What if they were having an affair in private or frequenting the bars? Aren't those traits more like the works of the flesh? And wouldn't those traits be more characteristic of a carnal Christian? Wouldn't that make said minister really just a carnal Christian and not a spiritual leader?

Not all who prophesy are mature. Not all who preach are clean. Not all who exhort are pure. I will repeat my point: the Gifts of the Spirit do not prove maturity. Balaam's *donkey* manifested three Gifts of the Spirit without being a prophet, a believer, or even a human being.[16]

---

[16] Balaam's donkey (a jenny or female) saw the angel (discerning of spirits). She spoke in Balaam's native tongue (gift of tongues). She spoke of their past together (word of knowledge).

On the other hand, the Fruit of the Spirit are lived where the rubber meets the road, in the humdrum of day-to-day life. Whereas the Gifts of the Spirit are a sprint, the Fruit of the Spirit (the real spiritual fruit) are an ultra-marathon. The Fruit of the Spirit accomplish their greatest work in private, away from the lights of the church service. It is in the comings and goings of the daily private life, away from the crowds and the public praise, where the light of our personal walk with Jesus Christ will shine for all to see. And what better way to describe the light of Matthew 5:16 shining in our lives than to substitute each of the nine spiritual fruit for the light spoken of in this famous Bible verse:

- Let your **love** so shine . . .
- Let your **joy** so shine . . .
- Let your **peace** so shine . . .
- Let your **longsuffering** so shine . . .
- Let your **gentleness** so shine . . .
- Let your **goodness** so shine . . .
- Let your **faithfulness** so shine . . .
- Let your **meekness** so shine . . .
- Let your **self-control** so shine . . . before men, that they may see your good works, and glorify your Father which is in heaven.

These are the *real* fruit that glorify God, and real fruit-bearing requires discipleship. But discipleship requires discipline and very few Christians like discipline. Even fewer Christians are capable of self-discipline. Self-discipline requires a tremendous amount of self-control. And so the purpose of this book is to reacquaint the American Church with the missing Fruit of the Spirit—self-control.

Fruit Production In Our Lives

These supernatural fruit are produced when the Christian allows the Holy Spirit to work in their private life. Since the Bible describes them as fruit, understanding natural horticulture can help us grasp what it takes to develop them in our lives. If we want the Fruit of the Spirit, let us look to the natural pattern of fruit farming. In the natural, there is no such thing as instant fruit. Fruit does not grow overnight. Fruit production is a tedious, multi-step process. Simply described, it requires plowing, sowing, planting, watering, cultivating, then harvesting.

To begin, we must break up the fallow ground of our heart. This would be any area where we lack divine fruit production. We break up the uncultivated heart by praying for this area of our lives. Honestly, even if the Fruit of the Spirit is not being produced in this area of your life, something else is.

After this, we must sow the seed of God's Word pertaining to the desired fruit. If we need to produce the fruit of longsuffering, we must sow the seeds of longsuffering, not the seeds of meekness or joy. We have not because we ask not, so pray for the fruit you are lacking.

Next, we must water it with the rain of prayer. Daily rain is preferable. Then we must give attention to the beginning sprigs and cultivate any weeds away from our precious planting. Jesus warned that many cares of this world could sprout up and choke out what has been sown. More prayer is then necessary followed by more cultivating and weeding.

Finally, if we have been patient and consistent, we will begin to see the Fruit of the Spirit manifest in our lives. Perhaps we've been successful in producing the fruit of gentleness toward the co-worker we really don't like. Praise God! That's a victory. Or maybe we've finally developed the peace we needed for that tough family situation. That's a victory too! But now here is the reality of the Gospel—God wants us to constantly produce, not just one Fruit of the Spirit, but all nine. And not just for one area of our life, like marriage, or friendships, or on the job. Oh no! He wants us to produce all nine Fruit of the Spirit every day in every arena of life.

Feels pretty daunting doesn't it? To realize that God expects us to produce nine supernatural fruit in every area of our life—every day! All of a sudden, keeping the 613 Laws of the Old Covenant doesn't seem so hard. Under the Old Covenant, God's people only had to obey outwardly. Under the New Covenant, God requires us to bear fruit from the heart *and* obey His commandments. If that seems a little overwhelming, be encouraged. God would be unjust to require something of us we could not possibly accomplish.

The Fruit Of The Spirit As Attitudes

Growing up in church, I always heard about the Fruit of the Spirit, but to be honest, I'm not sure what I imagined they really looked like or how to know if I really had them. I knew they were good. I knew they were noble. I knew they were desirable. I knew I should be able to quote all nine of them. I just didn't know what it really looked like to have them in my life.

It may help us to view the nine fruit as attitudes. An attitude is nothing more than the voice and aroma of our heart toward someone or something. If we have a bad attitude toward our boss, we would understand that attitude is really the aroma of our heart toward them. Whatever our heart is thinking, despising, embracing, rejecting, loving, hating, appreciating, or begrudging about that boss . . . it will come out as attitude. We don't like being around anybody with these attitudes, and we shouldn't be purveyors of them ourselves. And attitude has a spiritual aroma. God can smell it. Demons can smell it. Your boss can smell it. And truthfully, if you're honest, you can smell it too.

You and I both know when we have a bad attitude. We've been experts on attitude from our childhood, beginning when mom and dad commanded us to change our attitude or "I'll change it for you." This may have been an attitude of grumpiness, disdain, dissatisfaction, frustration, anger, jealousy, unforgiveness, lust, entitlement, etc. Regardless, mom or dad did not like the aroma that childhood attitude was producing in their home and they wanted it changed, one way or another. By the way, mom and dad were pretty smart because none of the aforementioned attitudes are biblically endorsed fruit.

Let us consider the Fruit of the Spirit as glorious and praiseworthy attitudes. I think if we will view the first fruit—*love*—as an attitude, it will really help us grasp what God is expecting from us. God wants each of us to possess a loving attitude. This would be an attitude that is characterized by everything 1 Corinthians 13 defines as love. This would make love a patient and kind attitude. Love is a humble and well-behaved attitude. It is an attitude that always rejoices at truth and righteousness. Love is an unfailing attitude. I think we get the picture.

We can apply this to *joy* and *peace*. Certainly the Fruit of the Spirit should be able to produce joyful and peaceful attitudes in the lives of Christians. A joyful attitude is much better than the grouchy, crabby attitude some Christians choose to walk with through life. A peaceful attitude is a far superior disposition when contrasted to a strife-filled agitated lifestyle.

The fourth Fruit of the Spirit is *longsuffering*. This is an attitude that is far greater than mere patience. Patience is the ability to wait. Longsuffering is the ability to wait while you are simultaneously enduring pain. Only the work of the Holy Spirit in a believer's life can produce the attitude of longsuffering.

The fifth Fruit of the Spirit is *gentleness* (*kindness* in other translations). I find it amazing that it takes the Fruit of the Holy Spirit to produce true gentleness. Certainly, having a kind attitude is preferable over being a jerk, and being gentle is a requisite for being a minister of the Gospel.[17]

The sixth fruit listed by Paul is *goodness*. Goodness refers to what is excellent, honorable, and distinguished. It describes the soul that flees guile, guise, and the desire to mislead people. The same word for goodness is used by Jesus to describe the "good ground" that gladly receives the Word and produces some thirty, some sixty, some one hundredfold. May every born-again believer yield to the Holy Spirit and manifest this *good* attitude.

The seventh attitude of the Spirit is *faithfulness*. This fruit seems to be absent now more than ever. Even Proverbs laments, "a faithful man, who can find?"[18] It's easy for mankind to be faithful to the things important to them, but the Holy Spirit will enable us to be faithful to the things that are important to God Almighty. Proverbs promises, "A faithful man shall abound with blessing."[19] Faithfulness is an attitude that promises to bless both in the spiritual realm as well as the natural realm.

---

[17] 2 Timothy 2:24
[18] Proverbs 20:6b
[19] Proverbs 28:20

The eighth Fruit of the Spirit is *meekness*. Jesus Christ commanded us to "Take My yoke upon you, and learn of Me; for I am meek and lowly in heart: and ye shall find rest unto your souls."[20] Meekness refers to a gentle teachability. The Holy Spirit desires to bind us to Christ's yoke that we might learn from His meekness and humility. The attitude of meekness promises a reward of rest for the soul. Is your soul constantly agitated, nervous, or exhausted? Apparently, pride is exhaustting. You may need to develop the fruit of meekness—gentle teachability.

The Attitude Of Self-Control

This brings us to the ninth attitude of the Spirit and the subject of this book: temperance or self-control. This is the little-discussed, almost never-preached, vastly overlooked, last Fruit of the Spirit. As we will discover in Chapter 3, the original New Testament Greek words used for self-control reveal that the Holy Spirit is not just interested in giving us miracle-working power on the occasional basis (as with the Gifts of the Spirit), but perhaps vastly more importantly, He wants to give us power over our own appetites on a daily basis.

Consider this: many Christians may never see the power of the Holy Spirit demonstrated through a Gift of the Spirit called the working of miracles, but they could easily see the same Holy Spirit manifest every day of their lives through a spiritual fruit called self-control. And truthfully, with the help of a little bit of self-control, many miracles and healings would be totally unnecessary due to the avoidance of many sicknesses brought on by the lack of self-control.

Self-control is the Fruit of the Spirit that helps us obey Romans 6:12-13 (NASB):

> **[12]Therefore do not let sin reign in your mortal body so that you obey its lusts, [13]and do not go on presenting the members of your body to sin as instruments of unrighteousness; but present yourselves to God as those**

---

[20] Matthew 11:29

alive from the dead, and your members as instruments of righteousness to God.

Paul stated that it was our individual responsibility to make sure sin does not reign supreme in our mortal bodies. The Holy Spirit will not do it for us, but He will help us if we will develop the fruit of self-control. We will see that the fruit of self-control is the help of God to enforce victory over the sin nature and its carnal appetites.

The Fruit Are Not Optional

Somehow the Body of Christ has developed the attitude that the Fruit of the Spirit are optional. Perhaps we have erroneously concluded that if the Gifts of the Spirit are not always present then maybe the Fruit of the Spirit don't always have to be present either. Let us be reminded of what Jesus Christ warned in John 15:2:

Every branch in me that beareth not fruit he taketh away: and every branch that beareth fruit, he purgeth it, that it may bring forth more fruit.

If we don't bear fruit, we are removed from the vine. Pretty straightforward. The Fruit of the Spirit are not optional. You either bear fruit or something is getting purged. Furthermore, a brief New Testament study will prove that Christians are actually *commanded* to produce all nine Fruit of the Spirit. Though Galatians 5:22 and 23 present the official list of the Fruit of the Spirit, other scriptures command us to walk in all nine fruit. Below is an example list. Notice how each sample verse is a command and not a suggestion:

- **Love** (*agapē*): This is My commandment that ye love one another (see John 15:12).

- **Joy** (*chara*): Rejoice with them that do rejoice (see Romans 12:15; 15:10; 1 Cor. 12:26; Gal. 4:27; Phil. 2:18; 4:4; 1 Thes. 5:16; 1 Pet. 1:6, 8).

- **Peace** (*eirēnē*): And be at peace among yourselves (see Mark 9:50; Rom. 12:18; 2 Cor. 13:11; 1 Thes. 5:13).

- **Longsuffering/patience** (*makrothymia*): Walk worthy of the vocation wherewith ye are called, With all lowliness and meekness, with longsuffering, forebearing one another in love (see Eph. 4:2; Col. 3:12; 2 Tim 4:2; Heb. 6:12).

- **Gentleness** (*chrēstotēs*): Put on therefore, as the elect of God, holy and beloved, bowels of mercies, kindness, humbleness of mind, meekness, longsuffering (see Col. 3:12). *heartfelt compassion*

- **Goodness** (*agathōsynē*): And God is able to make all grace abound toward you; that ye, always having all sufficiency in all things, may abound to every good work (see 2 Cor. 9:8; Gal. 6:10; Eph. 4:28-29; Col. 1:10; 1 Thes. 5:15).

- **Faithfulness** (*pistis*): Moreover it is required in stewards, that a man be found faithful (see 1 Cor. 4:2; Eph. 1:1; Col. 1:2; 1 Tim. 3:11; 2 Tim. 2:2; Titus 1:6).

- **Meekness** (*praotēs*): Now I Paul myself beseech you by the meekness and gentleness of Christ (see 2 Cor. 10:1; Gal. 6:1; Eph. 4:2; Col. 3:12; 1 Tim. 6:11; 2 Tim. 2:25; Titus 3:2).

- **Self-Control** (*egkrateia*): Self-control is commanded over 15 times in the New Testament, usually in conjunction with Church Leadership. The rest of this book will study this topic.

The Fruit of the Spirit are not optional. They are unlike the Gifts of the Spirit. We cannot control the Gifts, nor are we commanded to

true

Fruits Spirit & gifts of Spirit are "apples & oranges"

demonstrate them at all times. We are commanded to covet the best Gifts and to not be ignorant of them, but we are not commanded to produce them on a regular basis in our lives. They manifest as God wills. As previously stated, the only control we can exert over the Gifts of the Spirit comes down to either yielding to their manifestations and being God's conduit or quenching their manifestation and being God's frustration. The Fruit of the Spirit, on the other hand, are entirely our responsibility. God gives us the seed (the Word) necessary to grow the fruit and the water (the Spirit and prayer) necessary to nourish the fruit. But the rest of the work is our responsibility.

The Gifts of the Spirit don't prove our spirituality or maturity; they are the Holy Spirit showing off His power. If anything proves we are mature and spiritual, it is the fruit of God's Spirit working in our life daily. Truly mature Christians live a life defined by all nine "attitudes" of the Spirit. This book cannot cover all nine of those fruit, but we will thoroughly cover one: self-control. So, if you're tired of being *Fat, Broke, and Crazy*, read on to discover (or perhaps rediscover) the fruit of self-control and everything God expects you to do with it in your life.

CHAPTER 2

THE NEED FOR A CULTURAL OVERHAUL

Culture can be defined as the behaviors, beliefs, and total lifestyle characteristics of a group of people, transmitted from one generation to the next. Culture is seen in a people's attitude and behavior. It defines our reputation, whether it's a national reputation, church reputation, or even our personal reputation. Nearly every person on planet Earth is proud of their culture because it's all they know. And if we would be honest, we all tend to believe that our culture is the best. There is nothing wrong with being proud of your culture as long as it doesn't violate God's Word.

God's wisdom requires that we evaluate everything, including our culture, according to biblical standards and see how it measures up to God's Word. If we do this to Western culture in general, and American culture in particular, we must acknowledge that the American culture is not known for discipline or self-control. Sure, our business leaders are disciplined, as are our premier athletes and scholars, but the general population is not.[1]

As Christians, we are to live our lives according to sound Bible-based doctrines and not exclusively according to our national, regional, or familial cultures. We are certainly not authorized to exalt our personal cultural preference above the Word of God. Cultures are a dime a dozen and they must all be subjected to the Gospel of Jesus Christ. My dear Nigerian mentor once taught me, "God is not impressed with your American culture, nor is He impressed with my Nigerian culture. Brother, God has given us the Kingdom's culture!" The Kingdom of God

---

[1] Much of what is deemed "inequality" and "disparity" today can be directly tied to a disparity in discipline and self-control.

has a culture and we should personify it. It is a culture of salt and light. Though the Kingdom culture is thoroughly explained throughout the Scriptures, it is scarcely lived out in the West.

The Upside Down Kingdom

The Kingdom of God has often been called "the upside down Kingdom." Preachers have applied this descriptor as they have observed the Kingdom's counter-intuitive culture. So much of what the Bible teaches runs contrary to man's wisdom and experience. For example, in this kingdom, to save your life you must lose it. To gain the world, you forfeit your soul. To increase, you must give away. It is a kingdom where promotion comes through humility, while demotion is a result of pride. It is a kingdom led by servants, where the greatest achievement is self-sacrifice. Here the wise and the mighty are rejected, while the humble, weak, and poor are accepted. In this most unique kingdom, the slave is brother to his master and the king is called to serve the pauper. It is a kingdom where there is no respect of a man's person and where the only currency is faith in God. It is a kingdom where the noblest behavior is codified into a list of nine fruit, spear-headed by sacrificial love. In short, this kingdom, when preached or manifested, will disrupt any and every societal culture it confronts.

The Lord's Prayer[2] prepares the disciple to expect just such a confrontation between the Kingdom's culture and the countless cultures established in the earth:

> **And he said unto them, When ye pray, say, Our Father which art in heaven, Hallowed by thy name. Thy kingdom come. Thy will be done, as in heaven, so in earth.** **Luke 11:2**

This model prayer teaches us to pray for God's Kingdom to come and make earth look like heaven. It should be obvious that in order for earth to reflect heaven's nature, a lot must change. The effective fervent prayer

---

[2] Often referred to as *The Model Prayer*, it gives a pattern or model for all prayer. The Lord set forth this prayer after the disciples asked Him to "teach us to pray."

of Christians should be causing these changes in the earth: changes to individuals, families, churches, cultures, cities, and nations.

Jesus explained that the Kingdom of God is like leaven, hidden in three measures of meal until the whole lump was leavened. Like leaven in a lump of dough, the Kingdom should be changing everything it touches, beginning with our individual lifestyles. As the individual is changed, they will affect their circle of friends and acquaintances. This influence will then spread to the community. The community's influence will touch the city, the city will touch the region, the region the state/territory, and the state will touch and affect the nation—just like leaven in a lump.

In essence, the whole of a city, territory, or nation rests on the influence of the Church. But if the local churches are more of a reflection of the national culture, we have a problem. It seems as though the modern church has lost its God-ordained Kingdom culture. It is no longer pure light or salty salt. It has often been said, "The Church is not to be a thermometer that mimics popular opinion; it should be a thermostat that transforms the mores of society." Today, the American Church is more a reflection of the <u>new</u> America than it is a manifestation of Jesus Christ, the <u>Ancient of Days</u>.

Paul Confronted Culture

The preaching and teaching of God's Word cannot help but confront all culture that does not line up with the Gospel. Please note that not every aspect of every culture across the world needs confrontation or correction—only those aspects that are contrary to sound doctrine.

Let us examine the Apostle Paul's influence on the island nation of Crete. Paul's first trip to Crete was about 61 AD. As Acts 27 records, he was a prisoner on his way to Rome when the masters of the ship transporting him decided to seek haven there in order to avoid winter storms. His time in Crete as a prisoner would have been brief and confined. There is no evidence he preached or established any churches on the island, but he would have been acquainted with the people of Crete and their reputation. Some time after his release from prison, approximately 66 AD, Paul traveled back through the area and left Titus there.

Now consider Paul's epistle to Titus. The Apostle Paul set Titus as the pastor over the island nation of Crete about 66 AD. Titus was commissioned by Paul to "set in order the things that are left undone."[3] The first chapter of Titus gives us the two-fold method for stabilizing a local church and addressing that which is undone: 1) appoint qualified godly leaders for the churches, and 2) confront the wicked aspects of local culture. This is an ancient formula for church success every modern church must embrace. Look at Paul's description of the Cretan culture:

> **[12]One of themselves, a prophet of their own,[4] said, "The Cretans are always liars, evil beasts, lazy gluttons." [13]This testimony is true. For this reason reprove them severely so that they may be sound in the faith.**
> **Titus 1:12-13 (NASB)**

When addressing Crete's culture, Paul referenced a 600-year-old quote. Apparently, the Cretan cultural reputation hadn't changed in hundreds of years. Their cultural reputation was defined by three sinful traits. They were liars, evil, and lazy gluttons. This wasn't all they were known for, but it was a list of the top-three things God hated about their culture. This is what the Kingdom was going to confront first. The Holy Spirit had moved upon the Apostle Paul to exhort and authorize Pastor Titus to correct the Cretan believers by "manifesting His word through preaching."[5] If the Cretan church was ever going to be sound in the

---

[3] Titus 1:5

[4] The Cretan philosopher Epimenides of Knossos (ca. 600 BC) famously said, "All Cretans are liars." This statement is held as a "paradox of self-reference" or a "logic paradox," in this particular case, known as *The Epimenides paradox*. The paradox that arises is, if Epimenides is a Cretan and all Cretans are liars, then Epimenides is lying, his statement must then be false, and therefore all Cretans are *not* liars. Or taken another way, all Cretans are liars, except Epimenides who is presumed to be telling the truth, therefore all Cretans are *not* liars. If this is the case, Epimenides just misled the listener and is therefore a liar, so perhaps all Cretans *are* liars. The logical arguments that have been proffered both for and against the *Epimenides paradox* read something like Abbott and Costello's "Who's On First." Inconceivable!

[5] Titus 1:3

faith, these three areas had to be confronted. It was the pastor's job to address and severely reprove this culture's perversion.

Cultural confrontation, not cultural conformity, is still part of the pastor's assignment today. True shepherds are not authorized to use worldly culture as bait. Pastors are authorized and anointed by God to severely reprove and rebuke any aspect of any culture that does not line up with the Word of God. This is how they keep their churches clean from the contamination of the world constantly banging at their doors. Conversely, any pastor not regularly preaching against the sins and pitfalls of their regional culture will be complicit in its infiltration and their church's eventual compromise.

Churches Are Like Hospitals

Hospitals exist as a comforting focal point in every community. People know to turn to them in time of desperate need because they have a reputation and culture of sterility, healing, and help. Hospitals may be full of sick people, but they are not defined by sickness. They are defined by treating and repairing that which has been damaged by disease or injury. This fact should perplex us: how can a place filled with germs, viruses, pathogens, cancers, infection, and pain *not* be defined by these? Because the mission of a hospital and its patients is one and the same—beat sickness and leave healthy.

People humbly approach hospitals sick and broken; but if they submit to the hospital's authority and prescribed treatment, they will leave treated and probably better. Through submission, the infirm become patients of the hospital and qualify to receive the medical help they desperately need. If the patient continues steadfast unto the end, great healing can occur.

This is a good picture of the Church and must be our attitude concerning sin. We must gladly receive people who want the cure from their worldly sickness and infection. If they want the cure, then we can easily administer to them the washing of water by the Word. By submitting to the local church's authority and discipleship, they can become disciples and qualify to receive all the spiritual help they desperately need. If the disciple continues steadfast unto the end, great change can happen.

A hospital also exists to improve the patient's quality of life. Hospitals don't advertise what they do. They don't need to. Their reputation precedes them—they help sick people! If a hospital ever stops treating the sick it receives, word will quickly spread, and it will eventually be shut down and abandoned. If a hospital can no longer make a distinction between the sick and the healthy, the injured and the whole, or the ambulatory and the invalid—what good is it?

This is a perfect picture of the Church. A local church exists to improve the quality of life of every region. Pastors exist to heal that which is hurt, repair that which is broken, win those who are lost, disciple those who are converted, and *rebuke that which is wicked!* When the congregation has been salted, then people can go out and salt the community. But if a local church ever loses track of what is holy and what is wicked, what is sacred and what is profane; if a church can no longer judge between what is sound doctrine and what is heresy; if a church ever becomes ashamed of its assignment, it becomes nothing but a savorless, powerless social club. If a church loses its savor, it will be good for nothing but to be cast out and trampled. Like the community hospital, every local church should exist as a stalwart against the sinfulness of its local culture. Many churches have transitioned from the pattern of a hospital to that of a hospice. Instead of treating the cancer of wickedness, they have chosen to make their congregations as comfortable as possible as they die in their sins.

The Adullam Culture Shift

When David was running for his life from deranged King Saul, he fled to the Cave Adullam. While seeking solace and solitude, David soon found 400 men and their families gathered to him. The Bible describes this gathering of people as bitter of soul, distressed, and in debt. Somehow David became their captain. David suddenly found himself the leader of a decent-sized community of cave dwellers, but this was a community defined by a culture of distress, discontentment, and debt. Not exactly an ideal environment to raise children or really accomplish much of anything. The good news is that things did not remain the same. David changed those 400 men and in doing so, he changed the culture of Adullam.

David's leadership offered a better culture to his broken down kinsmen and they gladly accepted it. They submitted to him and he made them what he was—a warrior—and what they could never be on their own. With God's help, David managed to replicate himself 400 times over. David's leadership revolutionized the lives of every one who attended the little karst church called Adullam. For example, David killed hundreds in battle. Adino killed 800 at one time in battle.[6] Both Jashobeam and Abishai are credited with killing 300 men with a spear.[7] David was also a lion slayer and a giant killer. Benaiah caught the vision and slew both a lion and a giant, the latter with his own weapon.[8]

To be fair, not everyone caught David's vision and standard equally. Before he was finally coronated in Jerusalem, David had a standing personal army of 600 men[9] who had been through the "Adullam Process." But remember, originally it had been 400 men. Somewhere along the way David picked up 200 more men who were trained to be men of war—not remain men of distress.

When David and his men pursued after the Amalekites to recover their families, only 400 men were strong enough to fulfill the mission. David had to leave 200 faint men behind. This reveals a tiered rank and file of soldiers. There was a major group of 600 men, but then a stronger group of soldiers numbering 400. The Bible reveals an even higher echelon of men, even greater than the 400. This group of 37 mighty men of valor are named individually in 2 Samuel 23:8-39.[10] Above and beyond the 37 mighty men of valor were the three captains: Ishbaal (aka Adino), Eleazar, and Shammah—each of these men victoriously faced large hordes of enemies alone.[11] And finally, there was the captain of them all, Joab—David's right-hand man and nephew.

---

[6] 2 Samuel 23:8
[7] See 1 Chronicles 11:11, 20.
[8] See 2 Samuel 23:20 and 1 Chronicles 11:22-23.
[9] See 1 Samuel 23:13; 27:2; and 30:9.
[10] cf. 1 Chronicles 11:10-47
[11] See 2 Samuel 23:8-12.

Even though there was an evident pecking order of skill and ability among David's personal army—600, 400, 37, 3, and 1—none of these men remained distressed, discontented, or in debt. They were radically transformed from defeatists to conquerors. They carried with them the culture of the Cave Adullam. But it didn't stop there. Once David was king in Hebron, these men continued to leaven all of Israel. The Adullam culture spread. David's culture spread to his kingly army that was led by his personal army, and by it God used David to subject all of Israel's enemies and afford peace for the next generation—Solomon's reign.

This is all very reminiscent of what Jesus Christ was able to do with 11 of his 12 original disciples. These men were from different walks of life—fishermen and business owners, tax collectors and political zealots, ignorant and uneducated. Their personalities ranged from contentious (James and John) to boastful and rash (Peter). Yet, when examined by the Christ-mocking rulers, elders, and scribes assembled in Jerusalem in Acts 4, the religious leaders recognized that they had been with Jesus. The Lord had successfully left His mark upon those men. It was discernable to even the unbeliever. Annas the high priest recognized that the Kingdom's culture had made an impact on the two former fishermen standing before him.

Babysitters vs. Leaders

This brings us back to the need for good churches and good church leaders. If we equate the local church to the Cave Adullam or the mobile discipleship of Christ, then every local pastor should be like both Jesus and King David. Broken people should be drawn to the local church and the care and leadership of its pastor, but they should not remain broken. It should not matter what is wrong with a person; the local Cave Adullam should be a place of radical transformation. They may drag into a local church sick, addicted, perverse, and demented, but if they want help and are willing to submit to discipleship, in time they should march out victorious, clean, holy, and delivered.

I have come to realize that not every pastor is a leader. Some are simply congregational babysitters. Babysitters don't actually lead. They don't steer the home or call the shots. Babysitters ensure that the children don't harm themselves or others in the absence of mom and dad. Babysitters keep the children safe, the diapers changed, the bellies full, but they don't really discipline. They don't advance the family. They are more like a familial space holder. They are simply called in to maintain status quo until the real authority shows back up. Whether by ignorance, choice, or design, this unfortunately best describes many of today's pastors. Many pastors are not really advancing the Kingdom; they are only maintaining the status quo until men of real spiritual authority step back up.

I have a friend whose church has developed the reputation for being the church for vagabonds, outcasts, and fringe-types. And truly his church does draw such an eclectic collection of people. Though this is the purpose of every church and though every pastor should desire for their church to draw all kinds of people, my friend's church has a serious problem: his fringe-types, vagabonds, and outcasts are not changing. They are not being conformed or discipled into the image of Jesus Christ. They have managed to develop some queer unspoken social contract with the pastor that allows them to come to church and remain the same. This is biblically unacceptable and is an indictment against the pastor. He has permitted his Cave Adullam to be a headquarters for unbiblical culture and not a base of transformative Gospel power. Perhaps he's not really a David. Real Davids can't help but reproduce themselves everywhere they go. Perhaps my friend is more of a good-natured babysitter than a disciple-making Kingdom leader.

The American Culture

Part of the Kingdom's culture is self-control. This is nearly absent from America's culture today. America is not defined by self-control or even moderation. Nearly everything Americans do is in absolute excess. We don't just eat; we go to all-you-can-eat buffets. We don't even wait to be hungry before we eat. We are a society that carries snacks with us on the go "just in case I get hungry." We don't just get a soda; we get the 86-ounce Super-Duper Kidney Buster. We don't just watch television; we binge-watch whole seasons in a single sitting. We don't just have a credit card; we have five credit cards and four of them are maxed out. We don't just play video games; we live online with our gaming community. We don't just gossip; we live on social media. We don't just collect trinkets; we hoard junk. I know these may be extreme stereotypes, but chances are, if you're reading this book, you landed somewhere among these examples. Compare this to the testimony of the early Christians, who, according to Galen of Pergamon,[12] were "so far advanced in self-discipline and . . . intense desire to attain moral excellence that they are in no way inferior to true philosophers."[13, 14]

If you ever travel outside the United States and have the opportunity to discuss the American culture, *shrewd, disciplined, organized, austere, sensible, prudent, efficient,* and *meticulous* are not the adjectives you'll hear. What is our reputation? Chances are you'll hear words like *loud, opinionated, excessive, opulent, obese, wasteful, arrogant, brash,* and *rude*. This is not to say Americans are not liked, admired, or even respected; I just want to point out that Americans have a certain reputation and most reputations are self-inflicted.

Consider the three facts about America we mentioned in the Introduction. Though we have the most advanced medical care, we are among the sickest population in the world. Though we are the most prosperous nation in history, we are also the most indebted nation on the planet. And though we have the greatest universities and the highest rates of higher education, we have the greatest incidence of mental illness on earth. America is fat, broke, and crazy. And America is supposed to be the Christian nation. What signal does it send? What kind of testimony do we present when we claim to be Christian, but the fruit of our personal lives and the fruit of our national culture fails to confirm this? What kind of testimony do we have when our Christianity can't beat the basest of carnal desires? Where is the evidence of the new birth? We are supposed to be that city on a hill. What happened to our light? For too

---

[12] Galen of Pergamon, aka Claudius Galenus, was a Greek philosopher and the most accomplished physician of antiquity. He developed numerous medical theories based on the dissection of animals. He died approximately 210 AD.

[13] Durant, *Caesar and Christ*, p. 667.

[14] By "true philosophers" Galen was probably denouncing the popular Epicurean sect of philosophy of his day. The Epicureans believed that pleasure was the greatest good and sought the fullest enjoyment of all their senses. As such, Epicureanism can be considered a form of hedonism in that it declared pleasure to be its primary goal. The "true philosophers" sought out wisdom to aid in self-control. Philosophy literally means *love of wisdom*.

many Christians, the only difference between them and their pagan neighbor is their Sunday morning tradition.

The Cursed Fig Tree

America, or perhaps the American Church, may be more like the fig tree that Jesus cursed than we care to admit. Naturally speaking, unlike most fruit trees, a fig tree produces figs before it produces leaves. So for Jesus to observe a fig tree having leaves, He would expect to lift its leaves and find fruit.

Alas, in Mark 11, when Jesus approached the fig tree and lifted the proud leaves that deceitfully proclaimed, "We have figs, it's fig season!"—He was disappointed and angered. He answered the deceitful tree's false proclamation by cursing it, "May no one ever eat fruit from you again."[15] Now, it would never bear fruit again.

Does this not sound even a little like the American Church? Do we not boast our Christianity? Do we not boast our faith in Christ? Do we not boast our mega-churches? Do we not boast our Christian heritage? Yet when the Lord comes and lifts the leaves of our churches or the leaves of our private life, will He find the fruit He's expecting? It is past time for the American Church to realign its culture and values with the Bible. It is time for the American Church to divorce its carnal cultural predilections and embrace biblical Christianity again. We must embrace the Kingdom's culture. Self-control would be a great a place to start.

---

[15] See Mark 11:14 (NIV).

CHAPTER 3
SELF-CONTROL IN
THE NEW TESTAMENT

Many Bible doctrines can be classified as Practical Theology.[1] Practical theology refers to the Bible doctrines that can be implemented as personal practices. Not all doctrine can be reflected in a personal practice or lifestyle.[2] Of the myriad of Bible doctrines established and accepted, most important Bible-based doctrines may be those that can be immediately applicable to the believer today. Self-control is one such doctrine.

Self-control is the doctrine of self-mastery. It is considered "self" mastery because no one, not even God, can do it for you. God commands it, and therefore, He will grace us to do it. But make no mistake about it, if we don't master ourselves, no one else will. If we don't master ourselves, something else will.

If we understand man to be a tripartite being consisting of spirit, soul, and body, then the discipline of self-mastery must be applied to those parts that are unrenewed. In the new birth, the spirit of man is born-again and regenerated in the image and likeness of Jesus Christ. Positionally, the spirit of a born-again believer is seated in heavenly places in Christ Jesus. Our spirit-man is perfect. This would exempt the born-again spirit from the necessary discipline of self-mastery.

The soul of man is comprised of the mind, the will, and the emotions. It is overwhelmingly evident from both the Scriptures and

---

[1] Theology is the study of God based on the Bible. God and His Bible are studied from different perspectives. These include: Biblical Theology, Systematic Theology, Exegetical Theology, Cultural Theology, Historical Theology, etc.

[2] Generally speaking, some doctrines, such as angelology, certain aspects of eschatology, or even dispensationalism, can hardly be applied to everyday living.

individual experience that the soul is not redeemed in the new birth. The New Testament teaches us to renew our minds,[3] submit our wills,[4] and how to use our emotions.[5] The believer can expect their soul to suffer a steady barrage of fiery darts from the enemy. The *mind* wants to dwell on vile and godless things. The *will* flares up in waves of selfishness to pursue its own ambition. And the *emotions* are all over the place, from anger to zeal, from bitterness to elation, happiness to despair, all before lunch on any given day. The soul then is a work in progress. Unlike the born-again spirit, it does require self-mastery. It must be programmed and disciplined according to the Word of God.

The body is even worse than the soul. Paul called it a body of death.[6] The original Greek language makes a distinction between the sin nature, or the flesh (called *sarx* in the Greek), and the body of biology in which we dwell (called *soma*). The *soma* is not the believer's problem; it is the sin nature, the *sarx*, contained within the *soma,* that is the problem. If it helps, view *soma* as a vessel and *sarx* as an appetite. Our vessel is not what we fight to remain holy; it is the desires and appetites contained within the vessel that present us with snares, traps, pitfalls, and temptations. Restraining sinful appetites is also referred to as "keeping our flesh under."[7] This will be a constant work until the day our vessel dies. Our *sarx*, the appetites that constantly push the boundaries of sin, is what requires self-mastery.

Self-Control In The Greek

There are four words in the Greek New Testament used to build the doctrine of self-control. The benefit of understanding these original words cannot be overstated (though the proper pronunciation of these

---

[3] Romans 12:2

[4] Luke 22:42

[5] Emotions are neutral, but their use can easily become sinful. We are to love righteousness but hate sin. We are to rejoice at right and truth, not at iniquity (1 Cor. 13:6). We are to covet earnestly the best gifts (1 Cor. 12:31), but not covet our neighbor's possessions. We can be angry and sin not (Eph. 4:26). We are to love God and the brotherhood, yet it is still possible to direct the same emotion toward the world (2 Tim. 4:10).

[6] Romans 7:24

[7] 1 Corinthians 9:27

words is of little concern). I have decided to subject you, the reader hungry for change, to a chapter dedicated to a little bit of Koine Greek. I have endeavored to make this chapter as readable, understandable, and pain-free as possible. Please keep in mind that the Holy Spirit purposely chose these particular words to communicate to us the doctrine of self-control. These words reveal the power and ability of Almighty God available to us through the fruit of self-control.

The four words from which we build the doctrine of self-control are *enkrateia, sophron, akrates,* and *nepho*. We will look at each word in order to learn the nuances of biblical temperance and to understand how vital self-control is to the life of the believer. As a student of the Word, you will, no doubt, be very familiar with the scriptures that employ each of these words. God expects His Church to be disciplined and self-controlled, so please bear with me in this chapter as we examine the many definitions and rediscover the lost fruit of self-control.

Enkrateia

The first of our four Greek words is *enkrateia*. It and its various forms are used six times in the New Testament. *Enkrateia* makes its most critical appearance in Galatians 5:23, "Now the fruit of the Spirit are . . . self-control." *Enkrateia* means *to possess power or lordship over a thing*. It is therefore translated *mastery, control, restraint, self-control,* and *temperance*. This indicates that the ninth fruit the Holy Spirit wants to produce in our lives is one of self-discipline, self-restraint, and self-mastery. It is a fruit that grants the believer power and lordship over all appetites. This would also indicate that the believer's authority and dominion in Christ must begin with themselves. If you can't master yourself, you're probably not going to master life, and you can probably forget about commanding mountains.

To the ancient Greeks, this word described someone having control over all things, maintaining a personal freedom in the face of everything that clamored to enslave them through their appetites. Philo, a Jewish philosopher during the times of Christ, used the word *enkrateia* to describe "restraint in relation to bodily desires, especially sex, food, or idle chatter."[8] It is evident that the most common slavery Western Christians face today is bondage to their carnal desires (e.g. smoking, food, gaming, alcohol, social media, sports, entertainment, etc.).

As with many words, Greek and otherwise, there are multiple word forms or cognates—noun, adjective, adverb, and verb. *Enkrateia* is the same. The verb and adjective forms of *enkrateia* are also found in the New Testament and incorporate such definitions as *to exercise self-control, disciplined, in full control of oneself, to master,* and my personal favorite, *to have a firm grip on oneself.* These definitions help us understand how God wants us to master and be in possession of our earthly vessels and their countless appetites. It is clear that we must control them (both the vessel and its appetites). God wants us to have a firm grip on our appetites even as Paul stated, "that each of you should learn to control your own body in a way that is holy and honorable."[9]

Self-control is a major component of the Gospel's work in our life and a major part of the Gospel message. Paul preached self-control to the Roman Governor Felix in Acts 24:24-25:

> **[24]And after certain days, when Felix came with his wife Drusilla, which was a Jewess, he sent for Paul, and heard him concerning the faith in Christ. [25]And as he reasoned (disputed, preached) of righteousness, <u>temperance (self-control)</u>, and judgment to come, Felix trembled and answered, Go thy way for this time; when I have a convenient season, I will call for thee.**

Paul's sermon about "faith in Christ" is outlined into three sections: righteousness, self-control, and judgment to come. The first part—the "righteousness" portion of his discourse—would have involved the message of salvation and the righteousness that is available through Jesus Christ alone. The final part of his sermon—the "judgment to come" portion—would have been a warning of what is awaiting all men upon their death. That leaves the middle portion of Paul's sermon, the "meat" of his sermon, which involved the doctrine of self-control.

---

[8] TCBL Delta-Epsilon pg. 212, *Enkrateia* entry.
[9] 1 Thessalonians 4:4 (NIV)

Self-control is a huge part of the Christian faith. Self-control directly addresses how Christians are expected to live in between being born-again, the first part of Paul's sermon, and the judgment to come, the final part of Paul's sermon. This sermon cut Felix to the core and caused him to tremble, abruptly terminating the meeting. Evidently, the Roman governor's life, like many Westerners, was defined more by gluttony and gross wantonness than it was by discipline and self-control.

Peter also used the word *enkrateia* to describe a step in the process by which he taught Christians to mature spiritually. He begins a discourse in 2 Peter 1:4 by exhorting the believer to receive the knowledge of God in order to escape the corruption of evil desires by becoming a partaker of God's divine nature. From there, he presents a process that requires a step-by-step progression of building strong character in Christ:

> **Now for this very reason also (escaping the corruption in the world through lust), applying all diligence, in your faith supply moral excellence, and in your moral excellence, knowledge, and in your knowledge, <u>self-control, and in your self-control</u> perseverance and in your perseverance, godliness, ...   2 Peter 1:5 (NASB)**

These Christian character-building blocks are laid in a progression, faith being the foundational layer. From the top down:

- Godliness
- Perseverance
- Self-control
- Knowledge
- Moral excellence
- Faith

We see godliness is built upon perseverance. And perseverance cannot exist without self-control because self-control includes the ability to control one's emotions and therefore endure hardship. And we cannot have self-control without knowledge because knowledge reveals what is acceptable and what is forbidden. And knowledge is forfeited without moral excellence, which is rooted in faith. These are all interconnected, and each stands upon the other like bricks in a wall. It must be noted that godliness is built upon everything that precedes it, including self-control. Suffice it to say, it will be nearly impossible for a Christian to be counted godly without the demonstration of self-control in their life. Self-control is the power whereby we are able to "abstain from fleshly lusts, which war against the soul."[10]

Self-control (*enkrateuontai*-verb form) is also spoken of in 1 Corinthians 7:9 concerning sexual lust. Here, the King James translates it as "contain," as in "to contain yourself." According to most commentaries, here Paul gave permission to the Corinthian believers "who could not control themselves" and who "lack self-control" to marry, for it is better to marry than to burn with passion. At least this is the traditional interpretation of this passage, though I do find this contradictory to the rest of Paul's exhortations on self-control, patience, and self-denial. The thought of Paul giving license to "just hurry up and marry so you can jump in the sack" hardly harmonizes with the rest of his teachings. Granted, it may have been the best wisdom to give the thoroughly debauched Corinthian church in that season. I can offer no other interpretation at this time.

The only other use of *enkrateia* is found in a powerful allusion to athletics in 1 Corinthians 9:24-27 (NASB):

> **[24]Do you not know that those who run in a race all run, but only one receives the prize? Run in such a way that you may win. [25]Everyone who competes in the games exercises self-control in all things. They then do it to receive a perishable wreath, but we an imperishable. [26]Therefore I run in such a way, as not without aim; I box in such a way, as not beating the air; [27]but I discipline my body and make it my slave, so that, after I have preached to others, I myself will not be disqualified.**

---

[10] 1 Peter 2:11

It is quite clear that God intends for us to be just as disciplined and self-controlled in our spiritual walk as professional athletes are in their training. Furthermore, Paul revealed that failing to keep our body disciplined and enslaved could result in spiritual disqualification. Do you see that? An undisciplined natural life can result in a spiritual disqualification! Another Greek translation says, "found unfit for service." Self-control is critical to our life if we want to be found fit for God's service.

This question of being fit or unfit for service is confirmed by the final usage of this form of self-control (*enkrates*-adjective) found in Titus 1:8 as part of the criteria for church leaders. A church elder or bishop must actively demonstrate self-control in their life. Without self-control, a believer would not qualify to be a bishop/elder, for a mature Christian leader must be "sensible, just, devout, self-controlled."[11] The qualifications for the bishop's office listed in 1 Timothy 3 also include self-control, but there Timothy's epistle uses the Greek synonym *sophron*.

Sophron

Sophron is an adjective and root word formed by two other words: *sozo—to save or rescue* and *phren—the mind and parts of the heart*. It literally means *a saved mind*. Its meanings eventually expanded to include *chaste, prudent, sober-minded, self-controlled,* and *to curb one's passions*. *Sophron* has five other cognates and combined they are used 16 times in the New Testament.[12] Unfortunately, the King James Bible often translates *sophron* and its cognates as *sober* or *sober-minded,* misleading the modern student's interpretation of such passages. Our modern understanding of *sober* or *soberness* tends to infer an alcohol or drunken context. However, this is not the original meaning of *sophron*.

In the 4th Century B.C., Aristotle used *sophron* when contrasting the self-controlled man to the self-indulgent man and the disciplined man to the glutton. Aristotle's evaluation of *sophron* concluded the self-controlled man "desired what he should, as he should, and when he should." When our minds are saved or rescued, our bodies and appetites will follow. So then, self-control begins with a renewed mind.

---

[11] Titus 1:8 (NASB)
[12] New Testament *sophron* cognates include: *sophroneo (v.), sophronizo (v.), sophronismos (n.), sophronos (adv.), sophronsune (n.).*

Sophron is used only in the Pastoral Epistles to describe mature men and women of God.[13] This fact reveals that part of maturing in Christ must include controlling your natural appetites by rescuing your mind. Conversely, a lack of self-control is indicative of spiritual immaturity and a loose, undisciplined mind.

Sophroneo is one of two verbs formed from *sophron*. Its definitions also speak of moderation and self-control, with its main emphasis being "restraint," or "restraining one's passions and desires." It is used in Mark 5:15 to describe the condition of the Gadarene demoniac after his deliverance, i.e., "*sitting, and clothed, and in his right mind.*" When Jesus encountered the madman of Gadara, the tormenting legion of demons had driven him out of control. While possessed of demons he was wild, naked, and self-destructing. The work of Jesus Christ in this man's life brought about a fruit of self-control. No longer wild, he was now seated. No longer naked, he was now clothed. No longer self-destructive, he was now in his right mind. A right mind produces self-control.

Peter combined *sophroneo* and *nepho* (covered later) to describe a critical attitude necessary for effective prayer. The New Living Translation reads, "The end of the world is coming soon. Therefore, be earnest and disciplined in your prayers."[14] This exhortation on prayer declares that we must be both focused and disciplined in our prayer time. Focus and discipline are only made possible by the exercise of self-control. Do you have a daily prayer time? Is it scheduled? If not, self-discipline can solve that problem for you. When you do go to pray, how often and how long does your mind wander? Do you find yourself daydreaming or thinking more than you are actually praying? Mental discipline is what is needed to be earnest and effective in prayer. Paul also used *sophroneo* in Titus 2:6 to exhort the young men to "control themselves"[15] or "govern their passions,"[16] which is certainly a needed

---

[13] See 1 Timothy 3:2 and Titus 1:8; 2:2, 5.
[14] 1 Peter 4:7 (NLT)
[15] *The Simple English Bible, New Testament:* American Edition. New York: International Bible Translators, Inc. 1981
[16] Campbell, Alexandar. *The Sacred Writings of the Apostles and Evangelists of Jesus Christ commonly styled the New Testament:* Translated from the original Greek by Drs. G. Campbell, J. Macknight & P. Doddridge. Grand Rapids: Baker Book House. 1951 reprint of the 1826 edition.

exhortation for young men in every generation. The remaining uses of *sophroneo* apply the definition of mental soundness.[17] But remember, mental discipline precedes the necessary appetite restraint God requires of His maturing children.

Paul uses the noun *sophronismos* in his famous fear exhortation to Timothy, "For God hath not given us the spirit of fear; but of power, and of love, and of a <u>sound mind</u>."[18] The NIV translates *sophronismos* as "self-discipline" and the NASB simply uses "discipline." We have not been given a spirit of fear, but of power, love, and self-control. The exhortation is clear: the Spirit of God wants to produce a disciplined life so powerful it can even overcome timidity and fear. How encouraging to know God has given us the spirit of self-discipline. How hopeful to know we can beat any fear! Unfortunately, it also means we are totally without excuse if we are undisciplined in life.

Our study of self-control continues in Titus 2:4, where one of the jobs of mature women in the Church is to *sophronizo* the younger women. This is a verb meaning *to train in the areas of self-control, mental stability,* and *prudence.* The translations on this verse vary, but the general consensus is that a proper rendering would be, "that the older women are to train (*soprhonizo*) the younger women, developing in them the character of mental stability and self-control necessary to love their husbands and children." One translation even states, "moderate as to opinion." Accordingly then, mental stability and self-control are necessary attributes if one is to properly love their spouse and children. Therefore, manifesting biblical love requires mental discipline and self-control. Lacking either will result in emotional tantrums, marital fighting, and a miserable home-life in general.

Titus 2:12 contains another form of *sophron.* Here the adverb *sophronos* is used to describe one of three attributes the grace of God desires to develop in our lives. Along with uprightness and godliness, the grace of God teaches every believer to live self-controlled.

---

[17] See Romans 12:3 and 2 Corinthians 5:13.
[18] 2 Timothy 1:7

> **It (the grace of God) teaches us to say "No" to ungodliness and worldly passions, and to live <u>self-controlled</u>, upright and godly lives in this present age.**
> **Titus 2:12 (NIV)**

The Complete Bible Library Greek Lexicon states the following about the use of *sophronos* in this passage, "The entire word group coveys the idea of 'sane, sensible, in one's right mind.' It pictures a person who is well-balanced, who has all aspects of his life under control and in proper relationship." So then, self-control is not just a fruit of the Spirit; it's also a byproduct of a grace-filled life and it knows how to say "no" to ungodly desires.

The final cognate in this family is the noun *sophrosune*. We get our little-known English word "sophrosyne" from *sophrosune*. The English meaning is nearly identical to its Greek parent. The Greek word refers to "a basic attitude which alone makes possible certain concrete modes of conduct." Its main purpose is restraint through reason. It is an attitude that manifests as a life of moderation, temperance, and self-control. It is also defined as "mastery over the desires." Certainly we are to master our desires so that they do not master us.

The opposite of this word is *hubris*. The Greek *hubris*[19] is defined as *lack of self-restraint, e.g., pride, greed, gluttony, overstepping boundaries, avarice, etc.* Paul used *sophrosune* to defend the Gospel when he was accused by Festus of being mad through much learning. Paul proclaimed in Acts 26:25, "I am not mad, most noble Festus, but speak forth the words of truth and *sophrosune* (words that produce restraint, mental stability, rationality, and self-control)."

In defending himself, Paul defined both the nature and the ability of God's Word. He declared that the <u>nature</u> of God's Word is truth—absolute truth. He also proclaimed one[20] of the <u>abilities</u> of God's Word—it produces stability and self-restraint. God's words are words of absolute

---

[19] The modern English use of hubris has come to mean *pride* and *excessive confidence*.

[20] Other abilities of God's Word include healing (Ps. 107:20; Prov. 4:20-22), deliverance (Matt. 8:16; John 8:32), and cleansing (John 15:3). It also converts the soul, makes wise the simple, rejoices the heart, and enlightens the eyes (Ps. 19:7-8).

truth and self-control. In essence he was saying, "How can I be mad when what I'm declaring is truth, mental stability, and self-control?" So, we see that self-control is not just a fruit of the Spirit or a byproduct of a grace-filled life; it is also an ability imparted by God's Word.

Paul also used the same word to describe how godly women should dress when worshipping God, "in respectable apparel, with modesty and self-control."[21] I guess even in Paul's day the women had a tendency to overdo it and treat the House of God like a fashion show. Don't go overboard with nice apparel. It's one thing to honor the House of God with your very best; it's another thing to draw all the honor and eyes to yourself. For some, self-control may be necessary when it comes to wardrobe selection.

The final use of this word is found a few verses later in 1 Timothy 2:15, in what most commentators agree is the hardest passage in the Pastoral Epistles to interpret:

> **But women will be preserved through the bearing of children if they continue in faith and love and sanctity with <u>self-restraint</u>.**   **1 Timothy 2:15 (NASB)**

I offer no formal interpretation on this verse except to say the four characteristics of faith, love, sanctity (or holiness), and self-restraint should be every Christian's aim. And once again we see that holiness is impossible without self-restraint.

Akrates

Our third Greek word is *akrates,* which has as its root *krates* just as our previous word *enkrateia* does. It only has one pertinent New Testament cognate *akrasia,* and combined they are only used three times. *Kratos* is a noun meaning *force, strength,* and *dominion. Akrates* is an adjective that adds the negative particle *a* to *kratos,* and therefore literally means *powerless, no strength,* or *no dominion.* This word is used only once in

---

[21] 1 Timothy 2:9 (ESV)

the New Testament to describe the debased and carnal condition of mankind in the last days:

> **Without natural affection, trucebreakers, false accusers, <u>incontinent</u> (*akrates*), fierce, despisers of those that are good,**   **2 Timothy 3:3**

The King James Version translates *akrates* as *incontinent*. Modern usage of incontinent or incontinence is often applied to the inability to restrain natural discharges of urine and feces. When someone is incontinent in this sense, they require an adult diaper to contain their mess. Incontinent Christians make spiritual messes that also require cleanup. Most other translations render this word as *without self-control*.

Too many Christians fall into the category of living powerless over their own appetites and desires. This should not be a Christian's testimony. We may choose to live powerless, but do not be deceived—we are *not* powerless! Living powerlessly and being powerless are two different things. The first is a choice of will; the second is a fact of existence. The fact is that we have the Word of God and the power of the Holy Spirit dwelling in us so that we will never be powerless over our own appetites.

Akrasia is the noun form of *akrates* and therefore carries all of the adjective's meanings, e.g. *lacking self-control, incontinence, intemperance, lacking self-restraint*. This noun is only used twice in the Greek New Testament; once by Jesus to describe the hearts of the Pharisees and once by Paul to describe sexual temptation.

> **Woe unto you, scribes and Pharisees, hypocrites! For ye make clean the outside of the cup and of the platter, but within they are full of extortion (greed) and <u>excess</u> (*akrasia*).**   **Matthew 23:25**

Jesus upbraided the Pharisees for their hypocritical lifestyle. They looked perfect outwardly, but inwardly their hearts were filthy with self-indulgence. The Lord's severe rebuke reveals that excess and self-indulgence are sins that begin in the heart of mankind. Some have tried to justify excess and greed by labeling it as "God's extravagance." It could be that what they have dubbed "God's extravagance," Jesus still calls greed and excess. Preachers consumed by hyper-prosperity would do well to judge themselves concerning their *needs* versus their *wants*. And if their wants don't "commend themselves to everyman's conscience in the sight of God,"[22] it would be wise for them to change their wants lest they be lumped together with the self-indulgent and incontinent Pharisees.

Paul's only use of *akrasia* is limited to a conjugal exhortation:

> **Do not deprive one another, except by agreement for a time, so that you many devote yourselves to prayer, and come together again so that Satan will not tempt you because of your <u>lack of self-control.</u>**
> **1 Corinthians 7:5 (NASB)**

> **Do not deprive each other of sexual relations, unless you both agree to refrain from sexual intimacy for a limited time so you can give yourselves more completely to prayer. Afterward, you should come together again so that Satan won't be able to tempt you because of your <u>lack of self-control.</u>   1 Corinthians 7:5 (NLT)**

Without going into the subject of conjugal rights, the spiritual principle discussed in this verse is that any area in a believer's life lacking self-control will serve to open them up to greater temptation than normal. While most temptations originate in personal lust,[23] Paul discloses here that other temptations are much more powerful and can even be demonic in origin. Lacking self-control exposes our lives to these higher-order temptations. Where do you continuously lack self-

---

[22] 2 Corinthians 4:2
[23] See James 1:14.

control? Be prepared for demonically orchestrated temptations in those areas.

Nepho

Our final word that helps to build the doctrine of self-control is the verb *nepho*. It possesses three cognates[24] in the New Testament. Altogether, these four words are used a total of 11 times. When used literally, *nepho* means *to drink no wine,* but when used figuratively it means *to be soberminded.* All New Testament uses of *nepho* apply the figurative definitions, not the literal. *Nepho* is usually translated as "sober" in the King James, once again making it difficult for the modern Bible student to understand what God is saying. Like the other Greek words covered thus far, *nepho* has both a mental application meaning *free from all confusion* or *mental fuzziness,* and the physical application of *self-controlled, disciplined,* and *well balanced.* Again, we can see self-control beginning in the mind and attitude and manifesting in a disciplined lifestyle.

Paul taught that self-control (*nepho*) is a critical characteristic separating Christians from heathen and righteous lifestyles from pagan lifestyles. His first epistle to the Thessalonians is rather indicting:

> **[6]So then, let us not sleep, like the rest, but let us stay awake and <u>be self-controlled</u>. [7]For those who sleep, sleep at night, and those who get drunk get drunk at night. [8]But since we belong to the day, <u>let us be self-controlled</u> and put on the armor of faith and love, and a helmet of the hope of salvation.   1 Thessalonians 5:6-8 (CSB)**

Here we see self-control is key to overcoming spiritual slumber and spiritual drunkenness.[25] It is also critical if you want to put on the spiritual armor of faith and love which both require self-control.

After prophesying about believers departing from the faith by giving heed to seducing spirits and doctrines of devils, Paul exhorted young Pastor Timothy by saying:

---

[24] New Testament *nepho* cognates include: *nephalos* (adj.), *eknepho* (v.), and *ananepho* (v.).

[25] Many today are drunk with the cares of this world. See Luke 21:34.

> **But as for you (Timothy), <u>exercise self-control in every-
> thing</u>, endure hardship, do the work of an evangelist,
> fulfill your ministry.**   **2 Timothy 4:5 (CSB)**

The King James reads, "watch thou in all things," leaning on *nepho*'s "sober-minded" definitions, but the Christian Standard Bible goes with the "disciplined, self-controlled, well-balanced" definitions. With that in mind, Paul didn't exhort Timothy to pray and fast more. Timothy wasn't told to retreat from society to avoid the great falling away. He wasn't told to pray in the Spirit or groan in travail an extra hour each day to fortify himself against seducing spirits, nor was he told to study the Bible more fervently than ever before in order to prevent deception from doctrines of devils. No! Of all the exhortations he could have given to prevent apostasy, Paul simply said, "exercise self-control in everything," or as one of the original definitions said: *be well-balanced*. You can hear Paul's desperate plea to his beloved son, "Don't fall away, Son. Don't give heed. Exercise self-control. Just be disciplined." What is one of the keys to avoiding the multitude of pitfalls and distractions seeking to pull us away from our faith in Jesus Christ? Self-control.

Peter also used *nepho* in his first epistle. Here it is used to paint a tremendous picture for how this word should be applied to our mental discipline:

> **Wherefore <u>gird up the loins of your mind, be sober</u>
> (*nepho*), and hope to the end for the grace that is to be
> brought unto you at the revelation of Jesus Christ;**
>   **1 Peter 1:13**

In this verse, sober (*nepho*) is preceded by a powerful cultural reference that beautifully illustrates what Peter meant when he used the word *nepho*. To "gird up the loins of your mind" is a metaphor derived from the common practice in ancient times of an individual taking their long robe, wrapping it close to their body, then binding it with their belt. This was done in preparation for any work or lengthy journey in order to remove any encumbrances to movement and maximize efficiency. This is exactly what Elijah did before he outran Ahab's chariot.[26] To "gird up the loins" of our mind is to organize and discipline one's mind in preparation for the task at hand. This is what it means to be *nepho*, sober-minded, disciplined, well-balanced, and organized in thought-life.

Ephesians 6:14a uses similar imagery to add another ingredient to the disciplined mind—truth: "Stand therefore, having your loins girt about with truth, . . ." The truth of God's Word is the belt that we use to gird up or discipline the loins of our mind. Only God's truth can keep our minds from falling apart. Romans 12:2 calls this the renewing of our mind.

Peter uses *nepho* twice more: once to describe severe biblical prayer in 1 Peter 4:7 and once as a key to avoid being taken by the devil's lion-like hunting skills in 1 Peter 5:8.

Ananepho is a verb that implies "coming to one's senses." In 2 Timothy 2:25-26, Timothy was commanded to instruct those who oppose themselves that they might "recover themselves out of the snare of the devil." From this we see that self-recovery involves hearing the Gospel and then adopting a complimentary lifestyle. This has also been called "moral and ethical self-control." We maintain moral and ethical self-control by the constant washing of water by God's Word. When the Word of God is no longer heeded, morals and ethics are the first to suffer.

Eknepho is a second verb form of *nepho* and is used in 1 Corinthians 15:34. It has a much stronger connotation than the previous verb. *The Complete Biblical Library* translates it as *Get sober out of your drunken condition!* The King James translates it as, "Awake to righteousness, and sin not." This verse implies that undisciplined Christians fall into sin and spiritual slumber. As a command, this imperative indicates we are capable of sobering our minds. This is self-control enforced upon the mind.

Finally, *nephaleos* is the adjective describing anyone or anything that is *nephos*. If someone is *nephaleos,* they are temperate and sober. Figuratively, they are free from rash thinking and hasty judgment, thus they are clearheaded. Literally, they are free from wine and intoxication. Once more, we see how self-control begins with mental discipline. The three uses for *nephaleos* are found in the Pastoral Epistles[27] and are used

---

[26] 1 Kings 18:46. See also 2 Kings 4:29 and 9:1.
[27] See 1 Timothy 3:2, 11 and Titus 2:2.

in the lists of criteria for church leaders and mature saints. Mature leaders must be stable in their thinking and patient in judgment.

Summary

We have covered four Koine Greek words that, collectively, are used 36 times in the New Testament. Seventeen out of 36 uses are found in the Pastoral Epistles.[28] This reveals that one of the major themes of those three epistles is the admonishing of the entire Body of Christ (not just leaders) toward self-control. Pastors should personify self-control. In doing so, they will help reproduce it in their congregations. Self-control is a critical characteristic of mature believers. One of the major accomplishments of our new life in Christ is the crucifixion of our old man, and the nails holding us to the cross—self-control.

> **Knowing this, that our old man is crucified with him, that the body of sin might be destroyed, that henceforth we should not serve sin.**   **Romans 6:6**

The crucifixion or death of our old man destroys the body of sin and grants us victory over sin. We are no longer slaves to sin. To be clear, we can still sin if we so choose, but we don't have to live bound to sin. Salvation through faith in Jesus Christ has supernaturally liberated us from the binding addictions of sin. Learning to gain and maintain this supernatural victory over sin is also called sanctification. But we must ask, how do we manifest this life of victory over sin? What does it look like? It looks like the Fruit of the Spirit called self-control.

As a brief review of the Greek words used by the Holy Spirit in the New Testament, here is a list combining many definitions of our four primary Greek words. This list will provide us with an overview of what self-control should look like in our lives:

- Possessing power or lordship over a thing

---

[28] By definition, the Pastoral Epistles are the three epistles Paul wrote to Pastors Timothy and Titus, i.e., 1 Timothy, 2 Timothy, and Titus.

- Mastery
- Restraint
- In full control of oneself
- To have a firm grip on oneself
- To contain yourself
- To curb your passions
- Chaste
- To govern one's passions
- Mental stability
- Moderate as to opinion
- Restraint through reason
- Well-balanced
- A basic attitude that alone makes possible certain concrete modes of conduct
- Desiring what you should, when you should, as you should

Galatians 5:23 reveals there is a supernatural fruit we are expected to bear called self-control. Self-control is the power of God to enforce our victory over the sin nature. Self-control helps produce a spiritual alertness. Second Timothy 1:7 proclaims that God has given us the Spirit of power, love, and self-control. Titus 2:12 declares that the grace of God teaches us self-control. And finally, Paul proclaimed in Acts 26:25 that the Scriptures are words of truth and self-control. The Scriptures are clear: God expects His children to personify self-control and live disciplined lives.

CHAPTER 4

ON THE NATURE OF SELF-CONTROL

Self-control is not just a fruit of the Spirit; it is both a biblical mandate and a divine calling for every Christian. Self-control is the calling to live as a demonstration of the life and power of God—the calling to live victoriously over the appetites of the old nature. In many regards, self-control is just another way of saying self-denial. When Jesus Christ taught His disciples to deny themselves[1] and take up their cross *daily*, He was calling for a lifestyle of self-control. To follow Jesus, we must effectively abstain from, or deny, ourselves daily. This takes self-control. As Titus 2:12 affirms, part of serving Jesus Christ requires us to deny ungodliness and worldly lusts because these lusts war against the soul.[2]

Self-control is the call for personal restraint and self-denial. Self-control stands in opposition to hedonism. Self-control is the command to decrease that Christ might increase. Doesn't sound very American, does it?

Hedonism

Hedonism is the philosophy that the pursuit of pleasures and possessions, and therefore happiness, is all that matters. Hedonists live for what brings them happiness, even if it is only momentary happiness, doing whatever is necessary to avoid pain or discomfort. For a hedonist to pass up the opportunity to be happy, if even for a moment, is unthinkable. Like Solomon at his worst, a hedonist says, "Come now, I will test you with pleasure. So enjoy yourself."[3] It is anathema for a hedonist to

---

[1] See Matthew 16:24; Mark 8:34; and Luke 9:23.
[2] 1 Peter 2:11
[3] Ecclesiastes 2:1 (NASB)

willfully subject himself to discomfort. The Christian, on the other hand, is called to seasons of discomfort, suffering, trials, tribulations, and self-denial. Christian hedonism is an oxymoron.

A Christian hedonist is no Christian at all, but for many believers there is no happiness they withhold from themselves. They have never met a cupcake they could refuse—for cupcakes bring joy; or a dress that did not need to be purchased—because a new dress brings happiness; or a TV show that did not deserve binge-watching—because binge-watching is pleasurable; or another knick-knack that needed to be collected—because trinkets maketh happy. I think we get the picture. Is there anything modern man, specifically Westerners, deprive themselves of?

Western affluence has fed the new hedonism. America's Christian foundation has allowed it to know the blessing of God—which in turn has caused us to innovate and invent unlike any society before us. Our innovations and technology have afforded our citizens copious amounts of free time never known by previous generations. No longer do we have to plow all day for our food or hunt and trap for meat. Nor do we have to milk the cows for our milk or cut down trees for our warmth. The West no longer has to work just to exist (i.e. subsistence farming). We, in the West, work to have nicer stuff. But what has the Christian West done with its free time? Has the Western Christian taken advantage of their free evening to pray longer or study deeper? No. We fill it with entertainment. We fill it with things that make for happiness and pleasure, not with things that crucify the flesh and afflict the soul.[4] The Western Christian has pioneered a new hedonism, and without even realizing it, this neo-hedonism is following the pattern of Solomon's implosion.

Solomon's Hedonism

I know many readers will be familiar with the rise and fall of King Solomon, but here is a brief review: Solomon, the tenth son of David, became king at a young age (estimates are between 12 and 20). He was

---

[4] I'm not against entertainment per se, but the American Church needs more God, not more entertainment.

"the man of peace,"[5] being named by God with the promise of a peaceable kingdom (in contrast to his father's reign which was marked by constant wars necessary to afford Solomon his reign of peace).

Early in his reign, God appeared to Solomon in a dream and asked him what he desired. Instead of asking for riches, honor, the life of an enemy, or even long life, Solomon asked for wisdom and knowledge that he might righteously judge and lead God's people, Israel.[6] Because of his humility, Solomon was not only given wisdom beyond the ages, he was also given everything he did *not* request.

The Lord's covenant of peace with Solomon allowed for a generation of unprecedented prosperity for Israel, and much was accomplished under the leadership of Solomon. Following the Bible narrative, it appears everything went smoothly for many years. He ordained governors, prime ministers, and princes; his wisdom granted him fame to the surrounding nations; he hosted dignitaries and royal families for years and maintained wonderful peace agreements with them; he wrote 3,000 proverbs and 1,005 songs; he undertook massive building projects like the famed Temple of Solomon, a house for his Egyptian wife, and his personal house at Millo that took 13 years to build. He levied a workforce in order to build several defense projects, namely the walls of Jerusalem, Hazor, Megiddo, and Gezer;[7] he built numerous military supply outposts throughout Israel and even established cities for his chariots and horsemen.

Everything seemed to run smoothly for the wise king until 1 Kings 11:1, "But King Solomon loved many strange women, together with the daughter of Pharaoh,"—1,000 strange women in all. In his old age, they turned his heart from Jehovah and he worshiped their gods. He permitted their gods to be worshiped in the temple of his namesake and even built houses of worship for Chemosh and Molech.[8] Solomon's betrayal and wickedness demanded God's judgment, but we will get to that shortly.

---

[5] 1 Chronicles 22:9
[6] See 1 Kings 3:5-15; 4:29.
[7] See 1 Kings 9:15-23.
[8] See 1 Kings 11:4-8. Milcom the Ammonite god was also worshiped. See 1 Kings 11:5, 33.

We understand that horrific falls from grace don't just happen overnight. Some sort of transition had to take place in the life of Solomon. Somewhere along the way his heart began to depart from God. We must ask some questions of Solomon: How were such momentum, peace, and wisdom forfeited for such debaucherous destruction? How did a man endowed with so much wisdom get so recklessly stupid? Amazingly, Solomon himself confessed to how he fell from such a lofty place and the Bible records his confession in the book of Ecclesiastes.[9] The answer is pretty surprising. Solomon's downfall began when he cast off restraint and left the self-control inherent in the law of God.

Israel's Monarchal Laws

Deuteronomy 17:14-20 provided Israel with eight laws concerning the selection of kings and the limitations of their power. Two laws are given on how to select a king: 1) Israel can only appoint the man God picks as king; and 2) the king will not be a foreigner. The remaining six laws apply to the king himself: 3) the king will not multiply horses for himself; 4) the king will not permit Israel to do business with Egypt; 5) the king will not multiply wives for himself; 6) the king will not multiply wealth for himself; 7) when the king comes to power, he is to have his own copy of the Law made;[10] and 8) the king is to study the Law all the days of his life.

So much can be drawn from these eight laws of kingship, but I will focus on those that apply to our study of Solomon and self-control vs. hedonism. Several observations are glaringly apparent. First, when comparing the reign of Solomon to these eight laws, only the first two laws were kept, and that obedience belonged to Israel, not Solomon. Israel appointed the king God had chosen—Solomon—and he was not a foreigner. Unfortunately, Solomon never kept the remaining six laws.

---

[9] I have often referred to Ecclesiastes as *Proverbs, Pt. 2—I Messed Up*. The fact that it serves as Solomon's *mea culpa* is abundantly evident.

[10] The Torah is also called the Pentateuch or the first five books of the Bible. This law (Deut. 17:18-19) concerning the king's royal responsibility does not use the word *Torah*, but instead reads, "he shall write for himself a copy of this law on a scroll in the presence of the Levitical priests" (NASB).

We will pay special attention to the six laws that apply directly to Solomon himself (although they contain the wisdom of God that modern politicians would do well to obey). They are laws of implied self-control—that is, they act as a restraint on the king in the three major areas where all leaders are tempted. In essence, they were meant to be the bumper rails of accountability on the bowling alley of Israelite leadership. These laws were meant to prosper the king not hinder him. Remember, the opposite of the Law is not grace. The opposite of the Law is lawlessness. Lawlessness is self-destructive. Self-control is anti-lawlessness. Self-control is necessary in order to keep the commandments of God.[11] And the law of God shows us where and how to apply self-control.

Limitation Of Power

Abuse of power is a temptation common to any person in authority. In Deuteronomy 17:16, the power of the king's office is represented by horses. Horses were the, well, "workhorse" of military might until the Industrial Revolution and the advent of modern warfare. God was not against Israel's kings having a large standing army; it was the building of a personal army that God opposed because it represented pride and abuse of power. Israel's kings were forbidden from increasing horses for themselves and their personal endeavors. This law served as legal restraint should the king forfeit his self-control and begin to abuse his power.

As an example of this abuse of power, King Saul "took" strong and valiant men unto *himself*,[12] while in contrast the poor and broken down "gathered to" David and he trained them up to serve Israel.[13] Unfortunately, years later David got into pride over the army he had built and suffered judgment for it.[14]

---

[11] We may no longer be under the 613 commandments of the Law (collectively called the Mitzvot), but there are over 1,000 New Testament commandments for which we are still accountable. Over 200 mitzvoth are still commanded in the New Testament.

[12] 1 Samuel 14:52

[13] 1 Samuel 22:2

[14] See 2 Samuel 24:1-25 and 1 Chronicles 21:1-30. The fact that this was a military census is evident from two facts: 1) Joab and an unnamed captain of the host are tasked with it, and 2) the numbers given are in terms of "valiant men" who "drew the sword."

The second part of Deuteronomy 17:16 states that horses (or might and help) shall not be obtained from Egypt since God had said, "Ye shall henceforth return no more that way."[15] This was a law instructing all future kings to keep Israel from going to the world for help rather than turning to God.[16] The purpose of this law was to ensure Israel habitually looked to their God in time of need and not the heathen nations.

Solomon broke both of these laws.[17] He had 40,000 stalls of horses for his chariots; 12,000 horsemen; and 1,400 chariots. He even built cities just for these called chariot cities. In fact, in blatant disobedience to Deuteronomy's monarchal order to not "return to Egypt, to the end that he should multiply horses," Solomon imported his horses and his chariots *exclusively* from Egypt at a negotiated price. This rebellious business transaction was only natural since Solomon's father-in-law was none other than Pharaoh himself.

Not long after he was made king, Solomon formed a marriage alliance with Egypt marrying Pharaoh's daughter. Her name is never given, but she remained his first and primary wife even after he married hundreds more concubines. Not only was this marriage a violation of the Egypt prohibition, it was also a violation of Deuteronomy 7:3 which forbid intermarriage outside of Israel. Solomon lived a life in constant rebellion to the first two monarchal laws.

Limitation Of Libido

Sexual sin and politics have gone hand in hand from the beginning. Those in high authority often find they can have anyone they want, though that doesn't mean they should. Deuteronomy 17:17a set forth another law designed to act as a legal boundary should the king forfeit his sexual self-control. God commanded Israel's monarchs to refrain from taking multiple wives. This is a unique law because the scripture also reveals the purpose behind it: "that the king's heart be not turned

---

David's military might had increased from 400 weak men in the cave Adullam to 1.3 million valiant men throughout Israel.

[15] Egypt has always represented the place of destruction and slavery from which the Lord has delivered; the place from which his people should never return.

[16] See Psalm 20:7; 33:17; Isaiah 30:1-3; 31:1-3; and 36:9.

[17] See 1 Kings 3:1; 4:26; 10:28; 2 Chronicles 1:13-17.

away" from God or his responsibilities. This was a limitation of sexual appetite. Why anyone would want countless lovers or a harem is beyond me. A healthy monogamous righteous marriage is hard enough on its own. Any leader chasing numerous torrid love affairs, adulterous or otherwise, is a fool who will be too distracted to accurately serve his people and fulfill his office. The wisdom and safety contained in this simple law is boundless.

Of course, there are three things Solomon is remembered for: his wisdom, his temple, and his harem. His famous harem of one thousand women is another direct violation of Deuteronomy's monarchal commandments. Solomon admitted to building this harem in Ecclesiastes 2:8, "Also I collected for myself . . . the pleasures of men—many concubines" (NASB). The Bible clearly blames Solomon's failure on his wives' success in turning his heart away from God, but had he obeyed the law, there would have been no occasion for failure. If you're keeping score, so far Solomon is 0 for 3 out of six monarchal laws.

Limitation Of Wealth

Greed and politics have also been inseparable from the beginning. The king's office was ordained to lead the population into prosperity, not pervert the power in order to divert wealth into personal coffers. Proverbs 17:23 (NASB) says it well, "A wicked man receives a bribe from the bosom to pervert the ways of justice." Only God Almighty knows how many men have been made wealthy through their career in politics. This law of Deuteronomy 17:17b acted as legal restraint should the king forfeit personal austerity and embrace avarice. This law was a limitation of cupidity.[18] Unfortunately, Solomon also transgressed this law year after year[19] with the effect being recorded in 1 Kings 10:23, "King Solomon exceeded all the kings of the earth for riches and for

---

[18] Excessive desire, especially eager to possess something.
[19] See 1 Kings 10:14-15. Solomon's personal wealth grew 666 talents each year. The Hebrew talent (*kikkār*), borrowed from the Babylonians, weighed approximately 75 pounds. This is an increase of 49,950 pounds of gold each year. If we use the 2019 value of gold (approximately $1,400 per troy ounce), then Solomon increased his personal wealth by over $1 billion per year (in gold alone).

wisdom." Solomon confessed to this sin as well, stating, "I amassed silver and gold for myself . . ."[20]

God Without Limit

In contrast to the prohibitions placed on the king's personal power, libido, and wealth, (not surprising) there were no limitations placed on his hunger for God. Rather, the king was commanded *to seek* God and *to know* His Law. This is another common-sense law, because as it goes with a leader so it goes with their people, and when a national leader abandons God, chaos will fill the void. For this reason, God required every Israelite king to have his own copy of the Law and study it every day. This is the only law that is without limits[21]—power was limited, women were limited, money was limited, but the king could have as much of God as possible. God lovingly placed limits on the three things that are quickest to become idols: power, sex, and money. (Ironically, these are the same three areas that destroy preachers.)

God graciously explained His reasoning behind Deuteronomy 17:18's commandment, as well as the benefits of keeping this law. According to Deuteronomy 17:19-20, the benefits of knowing the Law are fivefold:

1. So the king would learn to fear the Lord (reverence).
2. So the king would keep all the words of the laws and statutes (steadfastness).
3. So the king's heart would not be lifted up above his brethren (humility).
4. So the king would not turn aside from the commandments (faithfulness).
5. So the king would prolong both his life and the life of his children (longevity).

---

[20] Ecclesiastes 2:8 (NIV)
[21] In jurisprudence, there are two types of laws: "affirmative duty to act" laws and "negative duty to act" laws. Affirmative laws mean you must do them and you are free to do them as much as possible. Negative laws mean you are forbidden from doing them.

These are still five great reasons to know the Word of God. There is no biblical evidence that Solomon either kept or broke these last two commandments. The Scriptures are simply silent here. I personally believe he walked with God for some period of time but not long enough to see the existing errors in his kingship. No doubt, had he kept the Law and continued in it, he would have eventually discovered these monarchal laws and been able to make the necessary adjustments. Regrettably, he did not align his private life with the Word of God and judgment eventually befell him.

Solomon's Mea Culpa[22]

The book of Ecclesiastes serves as Solomon's *mea culpa*. It is here that he revealed the mindset that led to his downfall. He writes from the standpoint of a man having everything only to lose it all. His analyses of *vanity* (it's discussed 33 times) and proffering of hindsight wisdom are summarized with the famous closing passage, "Let us hear the conclusion of the whole matter: Fear God and keep His commandments: for this is the whole duty of man. For God shall bring every work into judgment, with every secret thing, whether it be good, or whether it be evil."[23] It is in these two verses that Solomon reveals how he could have avoided all of his troubles—fear God and keep His commandments. It really is just that simple.

In the first two chapters, Solomon confesses to rejecting restraint and embracing hedonism. Read the following verses carefully. They are Solomon's confession and the key to understanding his downfall (all emphases are mine):

> **[16]I communed with mine own heart, saying, Lo, I am come to great estate, and have gotten more wisdom than all they that have been before me in Jerusalem: yea, my heart had great experience of wisdom and knowledge. [17]And <u>I gave my heart to know wisdom, and to know</u>**

---

[22] *Latin*: "my fault"; an acknowledgement of one's responsibility for a fault or error.
[23] See Ecclesiastes 12:13-14.

> **madness and folly**: I perceived that this also is vexation of spirit. Ecclesiastes 1:16-17
>
> I said to myself, "Come now, **I will test you with pleasure. So enjoy yourself.**" And behold, it too was futility. Ecclesiastes 2:1 (NASB)
>
> **All that my eyes desired I did not refuse them. I did not withhold my heart from any pleasure**, for my heart was pleased because of all my labor and this was my reward for all my labor. Ecclesiastes 2:10 (NASB)

After 20 years of building projects,[24] Solomon got bored and allowed himself to explore some dark places. After coming to a place of great wealth and prominence, having nothing more to want or get, Solomon purposely set his heart to know madness *and* folly; to test himself with all pleasures; to withhold no pleasure from himself. His justification for all of this is given in verse 10: *I have worked so hard; I deserve some rest and relaxation. I have earned the right to cast off restraint.* This eerily sounds like the modern mindset. It may even be your mindset.

I find the most horrifying statement of his confession in Ecclesiastes 2:9b, "also my wisdom remained with me." For all of his lawless hedonism, for all of his reckless debauchery—even while rejecting self-control—he still retained the divine gift of wisdom. He was still able to accurately judge Israel's hard cases.[25] Kings still came to see him and hear his wisdom.[26] The people of Israel dwelt safely and prospered all the days of Solomon.[27] He had wisdom for everyone, including himself. He just chose to ignore it. Solomon knew what he was doing was wrong, yet he did it anyway. I hope the lesson here is abundantly obvious: Solomon willfully rejected self-control, even when it was commanded by the Law, and chose to embrace lawless hedonism. His wisdom was not able to

---

[24] 1 Kings 9:10
[25] 1 Kings 7:7
[26] See 1 Kings 4:34 and 2 Chronicles 9:23.
[27] 1 Kings 4:25

salvage the kingdom from his rejection of self-control. Wisdom may be profitable to direct,[28] but self-control is required to follow those directions.

The Judgment Of Solomon

Solomon's judgment reminds us that sin still has a paycheck and that God will not be mocked—men reap what they sow. In His anger, God told Solomon that He would tear the kingdom from him and give it to his servant Jeroboam. For David's sake, the Lord left the tribe of Judah for Solomon's son Rehoboam[29] to rule, thus dividing the kingdom.

As if it were not bad enough to know that your sinfulness ruined your children's future and inheritance, God also stirred up two adversaries[30] to buffet Solomon and Israel the rest of his life. These were pricks in his eyes and thorns in his side—opponents he would never defeat. Solomon died knowing his lack of self-control had cost his family and his nation a great spiritual momentum from which Israel has still never recovered.

If we look at Solomon's downfall from another perspective, it was his hedonism that introduced Israel to the demon worship and idolatry only Babylonian Captivity would cure them of. King Saul never worshiped idols (though he did consult the witch at Endor).[31] David certainly never dabbled in idolatry or paganism. It was Solomon who opened Israel's doors to national idolatry. This was a national sin that took over 340 years to beat. Israel was only purged of national idolatry after 70 years of captivity in Babylon and Persia.

---

[28] Ecclesiastes 10:10

[29] For an Israelite king with over 1,000 lovers, the Bible is unusually silent on Solomon's offspring. Only three children are named: his son Rehoboam and two daughters, Taphath and Basemath (1 Kings 4:11, 15). The speculation behind this is grotesque: Solomon's concubines were devout worshipers of many other gods, including Molech (Ammonite god), Milcom (Ammonite god), and Chemosh (Moabite god). All three of these gods are considered one and the same and required infant sacrifice. So why aren't there hundreds or even scores of children in Solomon's genealogy? His many wives and concubines sacrificed his royal seed in the fires of demon gods.

[30] Hadad the Edomite and Rezon of Damascus. See 1 Kings 11:14-25. These men and their bands of soldiers did mischief against Solomon the rest of his life.

[31] 1 Samuel 28:7

But Wait, There's More!

Solomon's fall stands as a warning to us concerning the dangers of indulgence and release. If carnal liberation can undermine the supernatural wisdom of Solomon, what might it do to us? For this reason the Bible has much more to say about restraint and self-control.

> **Better to be patient than powerful; better to have self-control than to conquer a city. Proverbs 16:32 (NLT)**

Patience is a demonstration of emotional self-control. Proverbs declares that possessing patience makes you greater than a mighty warrior. But even greater than that is the possession of self-control. In the eyes of God, self-control is greater than one's ability to capture a city.

> **And put a knife to thy throat, if thou be a man given to appetite. Proverbs 23:2**

The mental image of a razor-sharp knife being placed to one's throat is an intentionally strong one. In such a scenario, perfect stillness is an automatic response lest one's movement accidentally cause the blade to cut back and forth on the throat and neck. The message is clear: if you are a self-indulgent person, do whatever it takes to stop it!

> **A person without self-control is like a city with broken-down walls. Proverbs 25:28 (NLT)**

According to Proverbs 25:1, this Solomonic proverb was copied out by Hezekiah's men. We don't know when this proverb was written, but it could very well have been after Solomon's great implosion. Either way, Solomon's admonition is clear: self-control serves as a great fortification for our life. Without it, we are easily plundered.

> **Moreover <u>when</u> ye fast, . . .**
> **Matthew 6:16 (emphasis added)**

Fasting is a call to self-control and it is a New Testament doctrine. Jesus said "when" you fast, not "if" you fast. Some would ask, "What should I fast?" To which I would answer, "Anything you crave."

> **¹²All things are lawful for me, but not all things are profitable: all things are lawful for me, <u>but I will not be mastered by anything</u>. ¹³Food is for the stomach and the stomach is for food, but God will do away with both of them. Yet the body is not for immorality (fornication), but for the Lord, and the Lord is for the body.**
> **1 Corinthians 6:12-13 (NASB)** (emphasis added)

Many would boast of their liberty and permission to do anything they want, even claiming they are "free" to do so. Paul stated that freedom ceases to be freedom when it masters and owns you. My pastor has always said, "Fast your attractions so they don't become distractions."

> **Mortify therefore your members which are upon the earth; fornication, uncleanness, inordinate affection, evil concupiscence, and covetousness, which is idolatry.**
> **Colossians 3:5**

Paul calls for an eradication of all sinful appetites. This is extreme self-control. The command to mortification echoes another of Paul's exhortations to "crucify the flesh with the affections and lusts."[32] This command presents us with the notion that we must exercise self-control on a sinful appetite until it simply dies. But how do we do that?

Self-control manifests as discipline, diligence, and consistency. We might say these three—discipline, diligence, and consistency—are the mechanics of self-control. If I walk in self-control, it will be evident by a disciplined, diligent, and consistent lifestyle.

When a Christian walks in the discipline, diligence, and consistency of self-control, the quality of their total life exceeds that of their neighbor. A self-controlled life accomplishes more. A self-controlled life

---

[32] Galatians 5:24

goes further, grows stronger, and endures longer. A self-controlled life will finish its race. The Bible has a lot to say about this power trio—discipline, diligence, and consistency. I will only hit the high points.

Discipline

A disciplined life is organized, ordered, and obedient. If we don't control our appetites, they will control us. It is very easy to yield to any appetite to the point of slavery. We must resist being in bondage to anything but Jesus Christ. This will take discipline. As one US Navy SEAL famously wrote, "discipline equals freedom."[33] Galatians teaches that it is for freedom we have been set free.[34] Self-control is the fruit of the Spirit that works to maintain that freedom and helps ensure we are not entangled again with any yoke of carnal or mental bondage.

Discipline, as applied here, means *to bring to a state of order and obedience by training and control.* God is the God of order and obedience. He is not the author of confusion. He expects us to be a human demonstration of order and obedience. Through His Word, He trains us and expects us to exert control—self-control.

Discipline can be brought to bear upon a system (or person) through either an outside force, such as a teacher, coach, trainer, parent, or by the system (or person) themselves, aka: self-discipline. A boss can ensure his company is a disciplined company. In a church, the local pastor can ensure his church is a disciplined church. At home, the parents can ensure their children and household are a disciplined household. But as you can imagine, in each of these examples, the business, church, or home will only be as disciplined as the respective leader. Sloppy bosses produce sloppy companies. Sloppy pastors produce sloppy congregations. Sloppy parents produce sloppy families. It is God's will for every believer to live orderly and obedient lives, producing order and obedience to God's Word everywhere they go. Two necessary ingredients for discipline are diligence and consistency.

---

[33] Willink, Jocko. *Discipline Equals Freedom: Field Manual.* New York: St. Martin's Press, 2017.

[34] Galatians 5:1 (NIV)

- What areas of your life still lack discipline?
- Reflecting on the definition of discipline, what will you do to bring order and obedience to that/those area(s)?
- Would special training in these areas benefit you?
- What are you waiting for?

Diligence

Diligence is the *persistent effort put forth to accomplish a task*. It is also the *unwavering exertion of body and mind*. Many people are diligent for a season, but few are diligent until the task is achieved. As Jesus taught, some people begin to build a tower, but don't see it through to completion.[35] The Hebrew word for discipline is also translated as *a strict decision* or *sharp*. Both of these definitions help us to see the necessary force behind diligence—diligence requires a strict decision and results in a sharpened life. Diligence produces a sharpness that cuts through the obstacles and opposition that stand between you and your goal. Diligence does not have time for fluff or excuses; diligence is going somewhere to happen.

The book of Proverbs contains five proverbs comparing diligence with laziness. To briefly summarize: laziness produces poverty, results in minimum wage careers, creates hunger, and has nothing but empty wants. Diligence, on the other hand, has the biblical promise of riches, promotion to leadership, stewardship of substance, abundant satisfaction, and plenteousness.[36] Laziness is the locust that wants to devour our destiny.

The Bible describes diligence with a beautiful word picture: setting your face like flint.[37] When your face is set like flint toward a task, it's as good as done.

- What areas of your life are still lackadaisical?
- What areas of your life are defined by dull laziness?

---

[35] See Luke 14:28-30.
[36] See Proverbs 10:4; 12:24 (NASB); 12:27; 13:4 (NET); and 21:5.
[37] Isaiah 50:7

- Since Proverbs promises that diligence promotes, in what areas of your life have you never seen the promotion of God?
- Since Proverbs declares that diligence brings abundant satisfaction, in what areas of your life are you unsatisfied or even frustrated?
- What will you do about it?

Consistency

Consistency is *steadfast adherence to the same principles, course, form, pattern, etc.* Christians should be the most consistent people on the planet. The principles and patterns we are to steadfastly adhere to belong to the Kingdom. They are found in the Bible and are therefore unchanging. Some Christians will adhere to the Kingdom's principles for a few days or a few weeks, maybe even a few months, but very few Christians are truly consistent for a lifetime. We ought to be consistent in our church attendance, consistent in our Bible study, consistent in our prayer life, consistent in our giving, etc. Some people are only consistent at being inconsistent. Their lives are consistently falling apart, never able to go anywhere.

Consistency means you are faithful to your commitments. Consistency means you are incessant in your goals and ambitions. Consistency is demonstrated in your resolve. We sometimes divorce consistency because we get bored with the assignment. Unfortunately, some Christians don't even have any goals. They simply live for the weekend. Without goals, our lives go nowhere and accomplish nothing. What a waste of a life! Seek God and set some goals. Then be consistent in achieving those goals. Resist boredom and embrace consistency to the glory of God Almighty!

- Are you consistent in your ambitions?
- Do you have a reputation for being stable and dependable?
- Are you still doing the last thing God told you to do?
- What will you do to change the inconsistencies in your life?

Spiritual Laws, Natural Laws

The natural realm is a reflection of the spiritual realm, and all of creation reflects the glory and counsel of God. This is evident in countless scientific laws from which, when both science and the eternal are compared, much can be learned.

There are four laws[38] of thermodynamics (thermodynamics being the study of the relationship between heat and mechanical energy). It is the Second Law of Thermodynamics that may help further explain the importance of self-control. This law is broken down into two parts. We will focus on the second part.

> *As energy is transferred or transformed, more and more of it is wasted; also, **it is the natural tendency of any isolated (closed) system**[39] **to degenerate into a more disordered state.***

Another way of stating the second part of the second law is: without the input of outside energy, a closed system will naturally deteriorate. Or, anything you do not work on will eventually fall apart.

Our lives are "closed systems." Because of the curse, everything in creation is naturally heading toward chaos and deterioration, including our personal lives. If we do not consistently apply effort, energy, and discipline, it will dissolve into nothing. Without self-control, we might dissolve into the pains of obesity or fall into the depths of poverty, revolving debt, and bankruptcy. Self-control is a divine call to constantly apply discipline to our lives, whether that be the discipline of a diet, the

---

[38] The other three laws of thermodynamics are: First Law—Energy cannot be created or destroyed. It can only change forms; the total quantity of energy in the universe stays the same. Third Law—As temperature approaches absolute zero (0K), the entropy of a system approaches a constant minimum. Zeroth Law—If two thermo-dynamic systems are each in thermal equilibrium with a third, then they are in thermal equilibrium with each other.

[39] By *system*, we mean any assemblage or set of parts, e.g. car engine system, human organ system, a house, a swamp. An *isolated* or *closed system* simply means that the system lacks the application or influence of any outside energy. The car without energy in the form of car maintenance will rust into oblivion. The body without food and water will die from malnourishment or dehydration. The house without repair and upkeep will become dilapidated. The swamp without fresh water will become anaerobic and die.

discipline of a regular sleep schedule, the discipline of investing in our marriage, the discipline of a financial budget, or the discipline of a fitness regimen. If you do nothing *with* your life, you will have nothing to show *for* your life!

Part of the Adamic curse was a divine promise that I believe instituted the Second Law of Thermodynamics.[40] Look at Genesis 3:17b-19 (NASB):

> **[17b]Cursed is the ground because of you; In toil you will eat of it all the days of your life. [18]Both thorns and thistles it shall grow for you; And you will eat the plants of the field; [19]By the sweat of your face you will eat bread, Till you return to the ground, because from it you were taken; For you are dust, and to dust you shall return.**

Before Adam's fall, creation was flawless and free from sin. There was no decay, destruction, or death. God's garden produced after its own kind freely, unabated, and without any effort from man. But after the fall, this all changed. God cursed the whole of His creation.[41] According to the verses we just read, this included the creation of thorns and thistles. The ground would still produce but not without "toil." Toil is the equivalent of outside energy being applied to God's closed system of a garden.

How is creation now a closed system? God cursed it. He cut it off from the life-giving power of His presence.[42] Just like He removed His glory from the bodies of Adam and Eve and they could see they were naked; God removed His glory from the Earth. Though He still manifests

---

[40] The First Law of Thermodynamics (matter cannot be created or destroyed) is demonstrated in Genesis 2:1 (NIV) "Thus the heavens and the earth were completed in all their vast array." This law is also called the Law of the Conservation of Matter. God was done creating new matter in the Genesis 2:1.

[41] See Romans 8:20-22.

[42] Numbers 14:21 and Psalm 72:19 call for a time when the Earth shall be filled with the glory of God again. Numerous psalms attest to God's glory being above the heavens and the earth (see Ps. 8:1; 57:5, 11; 108:5; and 148:13). Isaiah 6:3 is more accurately rendered "the fullness of the whole earth is His glory" (NASB, Young's Literal Translation, 1862).

His presence in the Earth, we understand it is not the same as it was before the Fall.

The moment God pronounced the curse, creation (and man) began to decay. After God's presence left Adam, it took him 930 years to physically[43] die. Likewise, God's special, pre-Fall presence has been removed from creation and it is slowly dying, even groaning in pain.[41]

Yes, God upholds all things by the word of His power, but that is speaking of sustenance, not eternal continuance. Sustenance speaks of God sustaining everything, which He does. Were He to retract His Word, every atom would cease to exist and creation would instantly disintegrate. As it is, creation is sustained but decaying. Now man must put forth tremendous energy and engineering to make anything work and last. This is why God will have to create a new heaven and new earth—one without the curse of sin still upon it.

Not surprisingly, we can find another reference to the Second Law of Thermodynamics in Scripture, howbeit a little more shrewdly stated:

> **By much slothfulness the building decayeth; and through idleness of the hands the house droppeth through.**   **Ecclesiastes 10:18**

How beautifully yet tersely put. This proverb evaluates two structures: a building and a house. Like the closed systems of thermodynamics, both the building and the house began as established and organized systems. But over time, without the input of necessary energy, both systems descend into decay and roof leaks.

This proverb is put forth, not as a reminder to literally maintain engineered structures, but to teach a spiritual principle. All of life requires the discipline of maintenance. The house can represent our private lives while the building represents larger institutions in our lives—careers, callings, ministries, etc. The warning is clear: just because we once put forth the energy and effort to build something great doesn't mean we can now take our ease. Without discipline, diligence, and consistency, our public lives will decay, and our private lives will leak.

---

[43] Adam and Even died spiritually the moment they partook of the forbidden fruit. God had warned them of this. See Genesis 2:17.

- What's currently falling apart in your life?
- Can you recognize any area where you are allowing the weeds of the curse to creep into the garden of your life?
- What are you going to do about it?

CHAPTER 5

SOUL DISCIPLINE
(HOW TO BEAT "CRAZY")

Beloved, I wish above all things that thou mayest prosper and be in health, even as thy soul prospereth.   -3 John 2

In classical Greek, the soul (or *psuche*) was understood to be the seat of a man's conscience and personality. It was held to be a distinct part of man (separate from his spirit and body). *Psuche* was also used interchangeably for any of the components of the personality. Hence, we understand the soul is made up of the mind, the will, and the emotions of man. It was also understood in the classic Greek that the individual had a responsibility over his own soul. This fact aligns with the Greek definitions of self-control, e.g., mental control that manifests as a disciplined lifestyle. Christians must exercise control and discipline over their mind, their will, *and* their emotions.

The Apostle John's greeting and prayer for Gaius in 3 John 2 encapsulates the doctrine of self-control found in the original Greek words as studied in Chapter 3. Remember, according to the Greek language, self-control is a discipline that begins with the heart and mind and is then reflected in one's outward lifestyle. As the Apostle John stated, success and health begin with a healthy soul.

To "prosper" in this verse implies far more than money. This phrase literally means *to have a good journey*, but figuratively, as is the case here, *to grant success in a matter, succeed in business affairs, to lead by a direct and easy way,* and *the good road.* Mental discipline is a necessity if you want to see the rest of your life flourish with "a good journey." Indecisiveness and mental confusion surely make for a difficult journey. A successful life and healthy body can *only* begin with a successful mind. Sadly, many today cannot claim to possess a successful or prosperous mind. Before we can master our flesh or our money, we must first learn to prosper our soul. In order to have a prosperous soul, we must discipline all three areas of the soul: the mind, the will, and the emotions.

Mental Discipline

According to the Mayo Clinic, mental illness is defined as a wide range of mental health disorders that affect your mood, thinking, and behavior. Examples include depression, major depression, eating disorders, anxiety disorders, schizophrenia, PTSD, and addictive behaviors. Mental illness will produce stress and an inability to function normally. The American Psychological Association reported in 2017 that 25% of U.S. adults have a mental illness and worse, nearly half of U.S. adults (150 million) will develop at least one mental illness in their lifetime.[1] Nearly half (45%) of those with any mental disorder meet the criteria for two or more disorders.[2] Furthermore, nearly 25% of all hospital stays in the U.S. involve mental illnesses.[3] To say mental illness has become an epidemic would be an understatement. Mental illness is not the will of God. The will of God is perfect mental peace.

> **Peace I leave with you, my peace I give unto you: not as the world giveth, give I unto you. Let not your heart be troubled, neither let it be afraid.**   **John 14:27**

These comforting words of Jesus Christ assure us that His will is for us to have peace of heart and mind. This verse also reveals there are two kinds of peace available to us: (1) the peace that the world gives and (2) the peace that only Jesus gives. Which do you judge to be the superior? Whether it is PTSD, anxiety disorders, eating disorders, or depression, peace is what is missing. Jesus left us His peace, but that doesn't mean everyone will take advantage of it. Sanity requires we take responsibility for our mind, will, and emotions. But how do we do that?

---

[1] www.apa.org/helpcenter/data-behavioral-health.aspx (accessed 7/2019).
[2] Ibid.
[3] Ibid.

> **Thou wilt keep him in perfect peace, whose mind is stayed on thee: because he trusteth in thee.**
> **Isaiah 26:3**

Though the will of God is perfect peace, the onus of responsibility is on the individual. Isaiah is clear, if we don't discipline our minds and thereby keep them on God, He will not be able to keep us in perfect peace. It takes a disciplined mind to stay focused on God and His promises. So what happens if our mind waivers off of God? The peace we so desperately need will waiver and possibly fade away as well. But if our minds—through discipline—return back to the Lord, the peace will return as well.

The Bible consistently teaches that God desires every believer to be self-controlled in their thought life. You can and must control your thought life. Your mind doesn't have to run non-stop. That may seem foreign to some, but it is completely possible to discipline your mind to the place where it will not just randomly think.

I like to use the example of a calculator. A calculator can be turned on and off. When you need help with math, you turn the calculator on, you enter the problem, press the equal button, and the answer is produced. When you have all the answers you need, the calculator is then switched off and placed aside. This is how our mind is intended to work. We instantly activate the amazing computer called our mind, input data, apply logic and reason, add a little bit of troubleshooting, produce an answer or perhaps several alternatives, make a selection, then turn the mind back off until it is needed again (generally 30 seconds later).

Some people, for many reasons, have developed minds that don't behave that way. They have minds that continually compute and add and subtract and divide and multiply and worry and fret and dream and scheme and con and fear and woulda-shoulda-coulda—non-stop. This often prevents them from even being able to sleep at night or focus during the day. This type of mind generally produces the right answers in life, but it also causes mental exhaustion, confusion, and even sickness. This is certainly not the will of God for anyone.

If you will learn to discipline your mind, it can become a valuable tool that only computes when you need it to. When you don't need it to, it will just sit there ready to be used like a good little calculator. I have personally found no greater Bible verse to help develop this kind of mental discipline than 2 Corinthians 10:4 and 5:

> **4(For the weapons of our warfare are not carnal, but mighty through God to the pulling down of strong holds;) 5Casting down imaginations, and every high thing that exalteth itself against the knowledge of God, and bringing into captivity every thought to the obedience of Christ;**

The mandate of this passage is very clear: every thought we have must be subjected to Christ's approval. In essence, Jesus Christ (the Word made flesh) becomes the filter for our thought life. If a thought is ungodly or unholy, cast it down! Paul uses some very aggressive terms when dealing with illegal thoughts. His uses of "pulling down," "casting down," and "bringing into captivity" imply an offensive battle, not a passive one. Disciplining your mind is a proactive job. If you don't do it, no one can do it for you. If you are going to discipline your mind, in the beginning it may need to be done nearly every moment of the day. But after some time of casting down imaginations and high things, you will find your mind being harnessed for your use, as you need it. Peace will only come after you harness your mind. Please hear me again: your mind does not have to run non-stop! You can bring it into submission. God commands us to discipline our minds.

Filters And Shields

God's Word gives us a powerful single verse from which to build a thought-filter. Found in Philippians 4:8, this will set your mind free if you will put it to use.

> **Finally, brethren, whatsoever things are true, whatsoever things are honest, whatsoever things are just, whatsoever things are pure, whatsoever things are lovely, whatsoever things are of good report; if there be**

any virtue, and if there be any praise, think on these things. Philippians 4:8 (emphasis added)

There are so many wicked things on which our minds can dwell, but the Holy Spirit forbids them all. This verse teaches us to use truth, honesty, justice, purity, love, goodness, virtue, and praise to build a mental filter that can help keep anything contrary to those from setting up in our heart and robbing us of peace. This doesn't mean we refuse to deal with or acknowledge the wicked things of life—certainly not! This passage teaches us where our minds should rest. Too often Christians allow their minds to constantly churn, wallow, and dwell on the foulest of things—all to no benefit. Mental self-control must be developed if we are to ever enjoy the fullness God desires for us.

The famous Ephesians 6 passage concerning the Armor of God also teaches mental discipline, emphasizing mental discipline over all the other components of the armor:

Above all, taking the shield of faith, wherewith ye shall be able to quench all the fiery darts[4] of the wicked one. Ephesians 6:16 (emphasis added)

There are six pieces to the Armor of God: the belt of truth, breastplate of righteousness, Gospel sandals, shield of faith, helmet of salvation, and the sword of the Spirit. But verse 16 emphasizes "above all" the shield of faith for the purposes of quenching the fiery javelins of the enemy. These fiery darts are mental attacks that come against the believer's mind.

Dr. Mark T. Barclay has often said, "Each of us has 10,000 thoughts a day. And some of them are actually ours." These thoughts include suicide, paranoia, fear, self-harm, hopelessness, quit, etc. Some of these thoughts could easily be classified as fiery darts. They are demonic in origin. These thoughts may or may not be our fault. Some we invited in by

---

[4] The King James' usage of "dart" can be misleading to the modern student. From the Greek *belos*, a projectile thrown. In combat, this referred to either an arrow shot from a bow or a javelin thrown by hand. Rome's enemies often used arrows dipped in pitch and set aflame. Here it must be understood to be a flaming arrow.

reading or watching things we had no business exposing ourselves to. Others simply come from being in this fallen world. However, once they are in our minds, though they may not be our fault, they are completely our responsibility. We must extinguish them by using the shield of faith and by speaking or praying against them. The shield of faith—our faith—should be built on the Word of God and the Philippians 4:8 filter. Without a disciplined mind, you will not have a disciplined life.

Personal Victory Over Purple Hippos

I am thankful that the Lord began to teach me about disciplining my mind when I was 19. I had just rededicated my life to Christ and was trying to serve Him with all of my might. The only problem was that my mind had been exposed to filth in my backslidden condition and these thoughts were constantly being burped up by my mind (for the sake of storytelling, I will call the specific filth *purple hippos*).

The purple hippos grieved my teenage heart and frustrated me. I could not figure out why I was having these thoughts even though I was now serving God, reading my Bible, and praying every day. In fact, the closer I drew to God, the more these filthy thoughts seemed to flourish and grieve my heart. The thoughts of purple hippos would burp up at the most inopportune time: while I was praying, while I was studying for college, while I was in church, while I was worshiping. Blah! I hated it. I began to cry out to God nearly everyday, "Lord, please help me. I don't know what's wrong, but the more I seek You, the more I have thoughts of purple hippos."

One day I wandered into the local Christian bookstore and, as an answer to my heart's cry, there was a book sitting on a shelf that called to me. It was as if God had reserved it there just for me. It was the book *Lord, Is It Warfare? Teach Me to Stand*, by Kay Arthur. Chapter 10 of that book taught me to speak the Word of God against any unwanted thoughts. It was this chapter that taught me about 2 Corinthians 10:4 and 5 and the command (not a suggestion) to bring into captivity every thought about every purple hippopotamus. I realized that if something was going to be done about these thoughts, it was my responsibility to do it!

From that time forward, every time I had a thought about purple hippos, I would rebuke my mind and tell it to shut up! I would say aloud, "Shut up, head! I rebuke you. I cast down every imagination and I bring into captivity every thought unto the obedience of Christ!" And then . . . my mind would have peace . . . for about 30 seconds. Then, almost as if in an angry vengeance, my mind would push back by throwing up a whole herd of purple hippos. So I would have to rebuke it again. And again. And again. And again.

I remember one particular day very vividly. I was in an Engineering 101 class—introduction to CAD design. I decided to count how many times I had to rebuke the thought of purple hippos. It was over 30. I spoke to my mind under my breath over 30 times in a 50-minute class. This taught me I must always have the last say with my mind. Then one day, before the end of the semester, almost without even realizing it, I was no longer having purple hippo thoughts. I couldn't pinpoint when or where they stopped, but they had. I recall pausing and trying to conjure up what a purple hippo even looked like and I couldn't. I couldn't find an image anywhere in my mind. I could not even construct one. It was like they didn't exist or if they did, I didn't know what they looked like because I had never seen one. Victory! My mind was finally free . . . of purple hippos. It took nearly six months.

I have since taught people that if their mind screams at them 1,000 times a day, they must rebuke it 1,005 times a day. Always have the last say with your thought life. This principle works on any kind of thought, desire, or emotion: suicide, premature death, divorce, sickness, paranoia, insecurity, fear, sexual perversion, temper, jealousy, etc. If you don't have a disciplined mind, you won't have a disciplined life.

Volitional Discipline

Man's volition[5], or will, gets him into more trouble than just about anything else. If we are going to develop a disciplined soul, we cannot leave out the will. And not surprisingly, the Bible also teaches us to discipline the will. A disciplined will is one of the most critical skills that

---

[5] The act of willing, choosing, or resolving; free exercise of the will.

can be learned in life. In fact, without a disciplined will the entire notion of submission is non-existent. All of life hinges on a person's ability to submit their will to every higher authority in their life. Even salvation in Christ depends on an individual's willingness to submit their will to God Almighty.

Every act of obedience requires volitional discipline. A person will either submit or rebel their way through life. Submission brings promotion. Rebellion brings pain. Authority is obtained through either submission to it or the theft of it. One of these makes you an honorable servant; the other makes you a tyrant or a Jezebel. These lessons must begin young. A bulk of parenting rests on a parent's ability to impart submission to their child. Parents must teach their child how to submit their will. In essence, parenting must effectively break the child's stubborn will without breaking their spirit.

Children, obey your parents in the Lord: for this is right.
Ephesians 6:1; Colossians 3:20

The opening of the *Lord's Prayer* teaches us to exalt the Kingdom of God and the will of God above all else, "Thy kingdom come, Thy will be done."[6] Jesus also demonstrated volitional discipline in the Garden of Gethsemane with His prayer of consecration, "nevertheless, not my will, but your will be done," or as Mark's Gospel states, "Yet I want your will to be done, not mine." [7] If we are going to be followers of Jesus Christ, we must follow in His footsteps and learn how to submit our will to the will of God. This is the essence of volitional discipline. The quicker a believer can discipline their will in the practice of obeying God—no ifs, ands, or buts—the sooner they will be able to make their way prosperous and their path easy.

In fact, the whole of the Gospel message requires the total submission of our will. Paul commended the Roman church for obeying "from the heart that form of doctrine which was delivered"[8] unto them.

---

[6] See Matthew 6:10 and Luke 11:2.
[7] See Matthew 26:39-42; Mark 14:36 (NLT); and Luke 22:42.
[8] Romans 6:17

Peter also addressed Gospel obedience in 1 Peter 4:17 and 18 (emphasis added):

> **¹⁷For the time is come that judgment must begin in the house of God: and if it first begin at us, what shall the end be of them <u>that obey not the gospel</u> of God? ¹⁸And if the righteous scarcely be saved, where shall the ungodly and the sinner appear?**

While the Roman Church was obedient to the Gospel and was commended for it, Peter ponders the outcome of those who don't obey the Gospel. The difference is a matter of volitional discipline. Peter noted that judgment must begin in the *house* of God, not the Body of Christ. These are two different groups of people. I believe this verse is differentiating between obedient Christians who can be found in the House of God and disobedient Christians who are rarely found there. Other verses bear out the fact that you can be a believer and still live disobedient to God.

Paul demanded of the Galatian church, "Who has bewitched you that you should *not obey* the truth?"[9] And later in Galatians 5:7, Paul asks, "Ye did run well: who did hinder you that you should *not obey* the truth?" We see that it is possible to be born-again and yet be considered disobedient.[10] Judgment begins in the House of God—the abode of the obedient believers. Peter then asks the hypothetical question, "What will be the end of those who are disobedient?"—by implication, those who choose not to be faithful to the House of God. Today, more Christians skip church than attend. If that is you, please hear how the Bible describes you: disobedient to the truth.[11]

Obedience is the act of a submitted will. You either choose to obey or you choose to disobey. Many Christians are so deceived and undisciplined with their wills, they foolishly think they can do what they want, when they want, as they want without any spiritual ramifications. They mistakenly believe Christianity is only based on what you believe and

---

[9] Galatians 3:1
[10] See also 2 Thessalonians 3:14.
[11] See Hebrews 10:25 (NET).

not how you live. Obeying God's will is a choice of your own will. The more you discipline your will to always say "yes" to the Lord, the more naturally it will come. There is a tremendous blessing in possessing a will that has been trained to obey the Lord. Rebellion is idolatry and stubbornness is witchcraft.[12]

Abraham disciplined his will to always obey God. A study of his life reveals he learned to obey God faster and faster with less delay as he matured.[13] His obedience brought great blessing to his family and his descendants. The Children of Israel disobeyed God in the wilderness and it brought great pain and suffering to them and their families.

Time and time again, the Lord blesses the obedient and punishes the disobedient. The Lord only seems to have problems commanding His people. Everything in creation obeys God but man. The oceans obey Him. The birds obey Him. The fish obey Him. Even donkeys obey Him. Only mankind disobeys Him. This is the result of carnal, stubborn, undisciplined wills. Part of disciplining our soul requires us to discipline our will. As Romans 13:1 states, "Let every soul be subject to the higher powers. For there is no power but of God: the powers that be are ordained of God." A subjected soul requires volitional discipline.

As a final encouragement and warning toward training one's will to submit to God, hear what the Word of the Lord says:

> **[19]If ye be willing and obedient, ye shall eat the good of the land: [20]But if ye refuse and rebel, ye shall be devoured with the sword: for the mouth of the LORD hath spoken it.   Isaiah 1:19-20**

---

[12] 1 Samuel 15:23

[13] Abram's first assignment had three parts: 1) leave Ur of the Chaldees, 2) leave all kindred, and 3) leave your father's household (members, estate, and wealth). Abram obeyed this three-part command in stages over a period of 11 years; first leaving Ur (Gen. 12:4), then he separated from Lot (Gen. 13:14), and finally he surrendered wealth to Melchizedek by tithing (Gen. 14:17-24). Twenty-four years later, at age 99, Abraham received the charge to circumcise himself and his entire household. He obeyed in the same day (Gen. 17:9-12; 23-27). Some 20 years later, God commanded him to offer Isaac as a sacrifice upon Mt. Horeb. Abraham took to the task early the next morning (Gen. 22:3-19). We see Abraham's assignments increased in difficulty, but he learned to quickly obey each time. God required a bigger sacrifice each time, from leaving comfort to sacrificing the son of promise.

God sees no middle ground. No shades of gray. There is either willingness and obedience or there is refusal and rebellion. A submitted and obedient volition gets to eat the best of what God has while rebellion is devoured and consumed away. I want to enjoy God's best. Don't you? What is the last thing God told you to do that is still left undone? What is your reason for rebelling?

Emotional Discipline

Emotions are the third and final part of our soul that we must discipline. You may find it liberating to know that every emotion found in the heart of man has its origin in the person of God. The Bible confirms this time and time again in its 66 books and 31,000+ verses. Consider the emotions the Bible ascribes to God:

- The **peace** of God (Phil. 4:7)
- The **joy** of the Lord (Neh. 8:10)
- The **wrath** of God (Ezra 10:14)
- The **jealousy** of God (Ex. 20:5)
- God's **laughter** (Psalm 2:4)
- There is a godly **sorrow** (2 Cor. 7:10)
- The **frustration** of God's grace (Gal. 2:21)
- The Lord possesses **hatred** (Deut. 16:22)
- The Lord has **pleasure** (1 Chron. 29:17)
- The Spirit **lusteth** to **envy** (James 4:5)
- He even experiences **pain** and **grief** (Eph. 4:30)

Since our emotions originate in God and are given to us as stewardships, it should come as no surprise that God's Word reveals to us how to use each of these emotions.

Reining In Your Reins

If you are a student of the King James Version of the Bible, you may have noticed it does not contain the word "emotions." Instead, the translators, using the language of their day, chose the word "reins." The original Hebrew word is *kilyah* and is literally translated as *kidneys*. This is its use when speaking of the fat and "kidneys" of the sacrifices given to God in worship. To the ancient Jews, however, the kidneys were also considered the seat of emotions. According to *The Complete Bible Library* Hebrew-English dictionary, "The inner organs were considered to be where one's real thoughts were hidden from humans, as external expressions could mask the inner life." With this in mind, consider that emotions are spoken of 13 times in the Old Testament. These verses confirm that our emotions can be: cleaved asunder,[14] consumed within us,[15] pricked with grief and conviction,[16] joyful and exuberant,[17] restrained by faithfulness,[18] far from God,[19] and pierced by the arrows of sharp words.[20] David even said his reins tried to instruct him after God had already given him counsel[21] (no doubt trying to talk him out of obeying God).

I'm sure every one of us can relate to this list as we have all experienced the gamut of emotional highs and lows. However, the most common statement the Bible makes concerning our "reins" or emotions is that the Lord God tries and tests them.[22] God never inspects or tests something because He's bored. The testing, trying, and inspection of our emotions serve a purpose—our betterment. This means we can expect God to correct us on the use of our emotions. Have you ever had the Lord correct your emotions? Was it because you rejoiced at something wicked or maybe you got angry at the truth? Are you prepared to let the Lord inspect more of your emotions?

---

[14] Job 16:13
[15] Job 19:27
[16] Psalm 73:21
[17] Proverbs 23:16
[18] Isaiah 11:5. Making a decision to be faithful will act as a tremendous stabilizer to emotions when they want to fall apart or get offended and quit.
[19] Jeremiah 12:2
[20] Lamentations 3:13
[21] Psalm 16:7
[22] See Psalm 7:9; 26:2; Jeremiah 11:20; 17:10; 20:12; and Revelation 2:23.

Controlling Our Emotions

Emotions have been given to us to express and experience life. Let me be very clear: emotions are not sinful, but what we do with those emotions can be very sinful. An individual is often deemed "emotional" when their emotions are out of control. We are created by God as emotional beings, but we should not be emotional in the negative sense. This is why we must also be disciplined in our emotions.

> **Patience is better than power, and controlling one's emotions than capturing a city. Proverbs 16:32 (CSB)**

Controlling one's emotions is better than being able to capture a city, though both require tremendous effort. For example, the Bible gives us directions on when we can and cannot rejoice,[23] and when we should and should not sorrow.[24] In fact, it is possible to be angry and sin not.[25]

> **Better to be slow to anger than to be a mighty warrior, and one who controls his temper is better than one who captures a city. Proverbs 16:32 (NET)**

Temper tantrums are hardly acceptable in toddlers, much less in mature Christian believers. The key to emotional control is to reject the notion that our emotions have to control us. This is a fallacy and a dangerous mindset. You can and *must* control your emotions—every last one of them. Study the Bible to learn how to accurately use them.

Love vs. Hate

A whole book could easily be dedicated to the subject of regulating and balancing one's emotions in line with the Word of God, but for the sake of time and book length, I will now only briefly compare and contrast love and hate. I have chosen these two emotions because the American Church has drifted so out of balance and is biblically illiterate with both

---

[23] See Romans 5:2-3 and 1 Corinthians 13:6.
[24] See 1 Samuel 16:1; 1 Corinthians 5:1-2; 1 Thessalonians 4:13; and Hebrews 12:16-17.
[25] Ephesians 4:26

of them. It is now common to hear Christians proclaim, "You can't control who you love." Lie. Or, "We're supposed to be lovers, not haters." Lie. How about, "God is a God of love, He doesn't hate." Lie. Or, "God is love and love wins." I'm not even sure what that one means, so . . . Lie.

Hopefully, we still remember that we are commanded to hate sin and evil,[26] but love our enemy (though we often invert the two). Actually, the Bible commands us to hate a lot more than we may realize. We cannot forget that God is not just a God of love, He is also a God of hate. As if to clear up any misconceptions, Amos 5:21 begins with a strong statement from God: *I hate*! I bet you've never heard that verse preached. God hates. He hates every abomination, idols, those that love violence, heartless religious routines, heartless offerings, and divorce.[27] Proverbs 6:16-19 lists the seven things God hates passionately: a proud look, a lying tongue, hands that shed innocent blood, a heart that devises wickedness, feet swift in running to mischief, a false witness, and anyone that sows discord among the brethren.

In the New Testament, the Lord Jesus revealed that He hates the deeds and doctrine of the Nicolaitans.[28] God is not just a God of love. He is a God who hates. This fact should not upset us. It should humble us to know that even though He hates the things we used to do (and some things we still do), He has declared His love to us through the atoning work of Jesus Christ. We cannot appreciate His love until we understand His hate, just like we cannot appreciate His mercy until we understand His wrath.

Some would argue, "Well that's God and He can do as He pleases, but we shouldn't hate." Let us be reminded that we are commanded to be as He is—holy. His hatred is a holy hatred. Regarding man's hatred, Ecclesiastes 3:8 states that there is a time to hate. The Psalms speak of "perfect hatred," what the NASB translates as "the utmost hatred."[29] This is a hatred David held toward those who hated God and rose up

---

[26] Psalm 97:10. Hating evil is actually a proof that we love the Lord.
[27] See Deuteronomy 12:31; 16:22; Psalm 11:5; Isaiah 1:14; 61:8; and Malachi 2:16, respectively.
[28] See Revelation 2:6, 15.
[29] Psalm 139:21-22

SOUL DISCIPLINE 85

against Him. We are instructed to hate suretyship,[30] lying, bribes, covetousness, every false way, and vain thoughts.[31] Even in comparison to our love for Jesus Christ, we must hate our own family.[32]

At the opposite end of the emotional spectrum from hate is love. This modern generation is obsessed with love, but not biblical love: postmodern, post-hippie, post-God love. It is the kind of love that Woodstock sired and ushered in a revival of rebellion and STDs. This is the love that has convinced a whole generation that you cannot control what you fall in love with. This is the kind of love that will not tolerate any hindrance to self-gratification. It is falsely assumed that this kind of love is an uncontrollable force of internal attraction—one that cannot be resisted, should never be rebuked, confronted, or restrained. It is basically the kind of love that embraces lawlessness and hedonism and dares you to disagree. To them, this kind of love is the supreme law of the cosmos and therefore justifies lawlessness. This is really nothing but selfish humanism trying to encourage itself in its cursed misery. What does the Bible teach?

First and foremost, the Bible very clearly teaches us that we can and must control our love. If it were not so, God would be unjust in commanding us what to love. It would be an impossible commandment to obey if love were not controllable. We are commanded to love God; therefore, it is possible. We are commanded to love our neighbor; therefore, it is possible. Husbands are commanded to love their wives; but mature Christian women must teach young wives *how* to love their husbands and children.[33] If God issued these commandments, we are more than capable of obeying—no matter what our hearts may feel or think today. God's commandments do not march us to our death or even to defeat. They march us into victory.

God goes so far as to tell us what *not* to love; therefore, that too is possible. The mature Christian has learned to love *neither* sleep nor this present world.[34] The mature Christian has learned to set their affections

---

[30] Suretyship, or suretiship, is loosely understood as cosigning on loans.
[31] See Proverbs 11:15; 13:5; 15:27; 28:16; Psalm 119:104, 113 respectively.
[32] Luke 14:26
[33] See Ephesians 5:25 and Titus 2:4 respectively.
[34] See Proverbs 20:13 and 1 John 2:15.

on things above and on the house of their God.[35] The Bible forbids the Christian from marrying an unbeliever.[36] This prohibition implies that believers should not fall in love with pagans. To even allow one's heart to do so sets one up for much pain. Second Corinthians 6:17 provides the escape plan when you feel your heart falling for someone off limits: "come out from among them, and be ye separate." Song of Solomon reveals that love can be awakened prematurely:

> **Do not stir up or awaken love until the appropriate time.**
> **Song of Solomon 2:7b (CSB)**

Love can be awakened prematurely and at inappropriate times. This verse assigns personal responsibility to each individual for the activation and timing of love in their heart. These verses demonstrate that love is controllable. You *can* control whom you love! We must regulate our emotions to ensure we love that which is holy and acceptable and hate everything God declares wicked and abject. This will take self-control.

David's Example

King David is a wonderful example of how to manage our emotions and just generally strengthen our soul. The beauty of David is that he was honest about what he was going through and what that was doing to his soul. It is encouraging to consider that Israel's greatest king had to fight discouragement and depression like we have to. Much of this is revealed in his psalms. It is easy to remember David as a mighty, fearless man of war, brutalizing his enemies, leading his armies against the enemies of God. However, a closer look at his psalms reveals not a calloused bloodthirsty warmonger, but a sensitive soul that had to quiet himself, seek God, and encourage himself in the Lord in order to obtain victory.

Consider that 23 verses in Psalms detail David "crying out" to God. Other psalms speak of his distress, his sorrows, his troubles and frequent anguish. Another 19 psalms speak of joy, eight psalms shouting for victory, and five psalms speak of laughter. It becomes very clear that

---

[35] See Colossians 3:2 and 1 Chronicles 29:3.
[36] See 1 Corinthians 7:39 and 2 Corinthians 6:14-18.

Psalms is a book filled with a full range of emotions from the depths of sorrow and despair, through the trenches of anger and vengeance, and upward to victory, joy, laughter, and triumph.

One of the keys to David's success was that he learned early in his life how to overcome discouragement. Discouragement slips very quickly into depression and despair. Discouragement literally means *to be deprived of courage, hope, or confidence*. The military debacle at Ziklag left him severely discouraged as he faced the threats of a deadly mutiny.[37] But David encouraged himself in the Lord and sought God for direction.

More than anyone else in the Bible, David practiced encouraging himself in the Lord. This practice is repeated again in many of his psalms. The psalmist begins many of his songs in desperation and emotional despair only to conclude with praise, victory, courage, and determination.[38] This is the secret to beating any discouragement, even its vicious big brother—depression.

The greatest example of David beating discouragement, depression, and despair is found in Psalm 42 and 43. He begins Psalm 42 literally crying day and night wondering where God is. Even those around him mockingly question him, "Where is your God?"

> **⁵Why are you depressed, O my soul? Why are you upset? Wait for God! For I will again give thanks to my God for his saving intervention. ⁶I am depressed, so I will pray to you while I am trapped here in the region of the upper Jordan, from Hermon, from Mount Mizar.**
> **Psalm 42:5-6 (NET)**

David recognized his depression and discouragement and refused to succumb to the silence so often accompanying this mental attack. He recognized depression as abnormal and unacceptable. He did not even give himself time to answer before he proclaimed the answer to himself:

---

[37] Oversight on David's part left the city of Ziklag without a military guard. David and his 600 men returned there to discover that the Amalekites had attacked it, kidnapping all of their wives and children, and burning the city to the ground. In their extreme sorrow, David's men spoke of stoning him. See 1 Samuel 30:1-10.

[38] Psalm 3; 13; 22; 42; 43; 54-56; 59-62; 69; 86; 102; 130; and 141.

"Wait for God. Hope in God, and give thanks to Him!" In verse 6, he declared what to do when depressed: "I will pray to God." Wow! How easy. The Bible way to beat depression and discouragement is to wait on God in prayer and give thanks to Him. This will require us to open up our mouth and declare the Word. This requires we not sit silent in darkness. Our mouths are hand-crank generators for the light of God. The more we speak, pray, confess, declare, worship, and praise *with our mouth*, the brighter the glory of God will shine about us.

David repeats this line of questioning twice more in the Psalms: in Psalm 42:11 and again in Psalm 43:5 for a total of three times. Each time he asks, "Why art thou cast down, O my soul? And why art thou disquieted in me? Hope in God: for I shall yet praise him." David took himself to task over the condition of his own soul. He blamed no one. He recognized it was his responsibility to encourage himself and get back after it. He also understood without the courage of God flooding back into his soul, things were only going to get worse. I don't think David allowed depression to hang around very long in his life. The moment he detected it, he attacked it with all he knew.

God saw it necessary to record this phrase three times for us. Let us use it to create for ourselves an emergency *standard operating procedure* (SOP) in times of depression or discouragement.

1. ***Why are you cast down, discouraged, sad, depressed, hopeless, _____, etc.?*** Recognize your soul is under attack and you lack the victorious joy God wants you to possess. Just be honest with yourself.
2. ***Why are you disquieted (humming) within me?*** Recognize that non-biblical thoughts have produced a great commotion in your soul. Take inventory of what you are thinking and begin to cast those thoughts down, telling them to shut up, even answering them with scripture.
3. ***Hope in God: for I shall yet praise Him!*** Open up your mouth and command yourself to do what you have known to do all along—hope in God and begin to praise Him.

Granted, speaking aloud to oneself can seem a little odd, but it worked for David time and time again and it will work for us. We will know the process has worked when a joyful countenance returns to our face, as Psalm 42:11 and 43:5 conclude, He "is the health of my countenance, and my God."

On The Nature Of Attitudes

We began this study with an evaluation of the Fruit of the Spirit as attitudes. Though we all understand what is meant by "attitude," it may help to take a closer look at the subject. To begin, the English language has not always employed the word "attitude" to describe what we understand as attitude. Other more archaic terms used to describe the same idea are *constitution,*[39] *temperament,*[40] and *disposition* or *mental disposition.*[41] Though the King James Version of the Bible does not use any of these words, the subject of attitude is very prevalent throughout the Bible, being evident in the original languages and captured in some of the modern translations.

The Hebrew word that captures the essence of what we understand as *attitude* is the word *ruwach*, which is translated as *spirit, wind, breath,* AND . . . *mental disposition,* or *the seat of emotions and mental acts. Ruwach's* equivalent in Greek is *pneuma* and it carries all of the same meanings, including *mental disposition.* Mental disposition is what we understand today as "attitude." So what exactly is attitude? Attitude is simply the voice of our heart. It is what our heart is saying about any given thing at any given moment. It is what our heart is thinking, feeling, and wanting at that moment. We know that we can change our attitude at a moment's notice when we want to. Sadly, it is usually easier to turn it sour than to turn it sweet. Attitude is the culmination of the three areas of soulish discipline we have just covered. It stands to reason, if we can discipline our mind, will, and emotions, then we can certainly discipline and control our attitudes.

---

[39] Character or condition of mind.
[40] The combination of mental, physical, and emotional traits of a person; natural predisposition.
[41] The predominant or prevailing tendency of one's spirits; natural mental and emotional outlook or mood.

Several modern versions of the Bible use "attitude" in translating the Scriptures. The following verses speak of submissive attitudes, judgment-worthy attitudes, new attitudes, proud attitudes, arrogant attitudes, rebellious attitudes, Christ-like attitudes, and different attitudes. Consider the following verses (all emphases are mine):

> But **my servant Caleb has a different attitude** than the others have. He has remained loyal to me, so I will bring him into the land he explored. His descendants will possess their full share of that land.
> **Numbers 14:24 (NLT)**

Caleb's faith is described as an attitude of loyalty toward God. May more Christians demonstrate faith that manifests as constant loyalty toward Jesus Christ.

> You should fear punishment yourselves, **for your attitude deserves punishment**. Then you will know that there is indeed a judgment. **Job 19:29 (NLT)**

Job revealed that sinful attitudes are worthy of God's judgment, not just sins of the flesh. Attitudes—those unspoken voices of our heart—can become so sinful that they invoke the judgment of God.

> And you, Solomon my son, obey the God of your father and **serve him with a submissive attitude**[42] **and a willing spirit**, for the LORD examines all minds and understands every motive of one's thoughts. If you seek him, he will let you find him, but if you abandon him, he will reject you permanently.
> **1 Chronicles 28:9 (NET)**

---

[42] What the King James translates as "perfect heart" the New English Translation renders as "submissive attitude." They are one and the same.

If Solomon was commanded to serve with a submissive attitude and willing spirit, then it *is* possible. We can change our attitude through self-control.

> ²⁵**But Hezekiah was ungrateful; <u>he had a proud attitude, provoking God to be angry at him</u>, as well as Judah and Jerusalem. ²⁶But then Hezekiah and the residents of Jerusalem humbled themselves and abandoned their pride, and the LORD was not angry with them for the rest of Hezekiah's reign.**
> **2 Chronicles 32:25-26 (NET)**

Hezekiah's proud attitude stood in opposition to the Bible's call to "humble thyself." Leadership pride is contagious. The residents of Jerusalem had caught their king's prideful demeanor. This brought the anger of God upon them as well. Thankfully, everyone repented. If Hezekiah could repent of his pride, so can we. We can change our prideful attitudes if we want to.

> **I will destroy anyone who slanders his neighbor in secret. <u>I will not tolerate anyone who has a cocky demeanor and an arrogant attitude</u>.**
> **Psalm 101:5 (NET)**

Pretty simple here. God does not tolerate cocky demeanors or arrogant attitudes.

> **Many times he delivered them, <u>but they had a rebellious attitude</u>, and degraded themselves by their sin.**
> **Psalm 106:43 (NET)**

> **<u>If you serve Christ with this attitude</u>, you will please God, and others will approve of you, too.**
> **Romans 14:18 (NLT)**

These two attitudes stand in stark opposition. The first attitude is one of rebellion while the second attitude is that of Christ-like servitude. At any given moment, we are either operating in one or the other. Which one defines your life?

> **[22]You were taught, with regard to your former way of life, to put off your old self, which is being corrupted by its deceitful desires; [23]<u>to be made new in the attitude of your minds</u>;**   **Ephesians 4:22-23 (NIV)**

The Bible teaches us to put off the old way of doing things and develop a new attitude. As this verse says, we "were taught . . . to be made new in the attitude of your minds." A new attitude is not only possible; it is actually expected of us!

> **So then, since Christ suffered physical pain, <u>you must arm yourselves with the same attitude he had</u>, and be ready to suffer, too. For if you have suffered physically for Christ, you have finished with sin.**
>   **1 Peter 4:1 (NLT)**

Here is another verse that doesn't just teach us to have a *new* attitude; it commands us to have the attitude of *Christ*. We *must* arm ourselves with the same attitude as Jesus Christ—one that is ready to suffer. This verse strips away any excuse we might offer as to why we can't change old attitudes or mindsets. If your attitude is not right, exercise self-control and change it!

The Big Three Mental Illnesses

Currently, mental health professionals identify three major mental illnesses: schizophrenia, bipolar disorder, and major depression. Current statistics tell us that 1 in 4 adults experience mental illnesses each year.[43] That means if you are reading this book, there is a good chance you may

---

[43] https://www.nami.org/learn-more/mental-health-by-the-numbers

have to deal with one of these three mental attacks at some point. Though I don't desire to go too deeply into this arena, I would be remiss if I did not offer a biblical answer to these life-crippling ailments.

Several years ago I studied "the big three" mental illnesses and their symptoms for several months as I taught my congregation on the Fruit of the Spirit. I made an interesting discovery that I will relate in the simplest terms possible. In short, most symptoms of every major mental illness have a polar opposite in one or more spiritual fruit. I believe maintaining the Fruit of the Spirit can work as a powerful inoculation against mental illness.

Major Depression

Depression (also called major depression or clinical depression) is a mood disorder that causes a persistent feeling of sadness and loss of interest. It affects how people feel, think, and behave. This can lead to numerous emotional and physical issues. Below is a list of major depression symptoms as adopted from the Mayo Clinic's website, followed by the fruit(s) of the Spirit that answer the symptom.

COMMON SYMPTOMS OF DEPRESSION
- *Sadness, emptiness, or hopelessness*—LOVE, JOY, PEACE
- *Outbursts of anger, irritability, or frustration*—PEACE, GOODNESS, GENTLENESS, SELF-CONTROL
- *Loss of interest in most activities*—FAITHFULNESS, LOVE
- *Anxiety, agitation*—PEACE, GENTLENESS
- *Feelings of worthlessness or guilt*—LOVE, JOY, PEACE
- *Suicidal thoughts*—LOVE, JOY, PEACE, SELF-CONTROL

Bipolar Disorder

Bipolar disorder, formerly called manic depression, is a mental health condition that causes extreme mood swings that include emotional highs (mania or hypomania) and lows (depression, with identical symptoms as Major Depression). What follows is a list of bipolar symptoms as adopted from the Mayo Clinic's website, proceeded by the fruit(s) of the Spirit that answer the symptom.

COMMON SYMPTOMS OF MANIA AND HYPOMANIA
- *Abnormally upbeat, jumpy, and wired*—PEACE
- *Increased energy or agitation*—JOY, PEACE, GENTLENESS
- *Exaggerated sense of self-confidence*—MEEKNESS
- *Racing thoughts*—PEACE, SELF-CONTROL
- *Distractibility*—PEACE, SELF-CONTROL
- *Poor decision-making, risk taking*—SELF-CONTROL, JOY, PEACE

COMMON SYMPTOMS OF DEPRESSION
- *These symptoms are identical to major depression. See the previous section.*

Schizophrenia

Schizophrenia is the most severe of these three mental disorders in which people abnormally interpret reality. Schizophrenia produces extremely disordered thinking and disorganized behavior. Admittedly, schizophrenia is not as easily confronted by the Fruit of the Spirit as major depression and bipolar disorder. Below is a list of symptoms as adopted from the Mayo Clinic's website, followed by the fruit(s) of the Spirit that answer the symptom.

COMMON SYMPTOMS OF SCHIZOPHRENIA
- Delusions (beliefs not based in reality)—PEACE, JOY, SELF-CONTROL
- Hallucinations (hearing or seeing things that don't exist)—PEACE, SELF-CONTROL
- Disorganized thinking—PEACE, SELF-CONTROL
- Abnormal behavior (disorganized behavior)—This kind of behavior includes unpredictable agitation, bizarre postures, dissociation, and even childlike silliness. These types of symptoms are indicative of deeper psychological issues and are in need of either deliverance or serious medical help.—PEACE, SELF-CONTROL

Conclusion

God's will is perfect peace. Soulish discipline requires constant vigilance. The chaos of the fallen world never ceases with its rhetoric, lies, and confusion; therefore, we cannot quit speaking and declaring the Word of God! No one can renew your mind but you. No one can harness your emotions but you. No one can submit your will but you.

- Do you judge your thoughts according to the Word of God?
- Can you see areas where your mind, will, or emotions might be out of line with God?
- Where does your will pull away from God's will?
- What are some areas in your life where your emotions get misused?
- Do you actively speak to vain imaginations? If not, when do you plan to start?

Minister's Moment

Ministers are the leaders of God's flock. We lead by example. A church will only be as healthy as its leader's soul. As such, our souls, (our minds, wills, and emotions) must be exemplary in discipline if we want our congregations to flourish. This means our minds must be kept pure from filth, our emotions must be in line with the Word, and our wills submitted to the plan of God. A minister's fall from grace begins with a compromised soul.

Many a ministry and minister have been brought down through sexual impropriety. But before a preacher ever commits adultery or any other form of sexual perversion, his or her mind first went there countless times. Perverse daydreams sow the seeds of infidelity. There will always be a harvest of judgment.

Other ministry leaders are emotionally unhealthy and are either grossly insecure and flounder as leaders or are dictatorial and heavy-handed in their leadership style. If your leadership style treads into the "jerk" end of the spectrum, remember, the Lord's servant "must not engage in heated disputes but be kind towards all, an apt teacher, patient, correcting opponents with gentleness."[44] If, on the other hand, you are insecure and emotionally tumultuous, don't forget, "faithful is he that has called you,"[45] and "the Lord is with thee, thou mighty man of valour."[46]

Finally, some preachers are just so stubborn and bullheaded, they're going to run their ministry the way they see fit, regardless of what God wants. They are going to preach when, where, and what they want—who cares what the Head of the Church wants. If that's you, please be careful. Submit your will to God. Be like our Lord Jesus Christ. Declare, "I have come to do Thy will, O God."[47]

---

[44] See 2 Timothy 2:24-25 NET.
[45] 1 Thessalonians 5:24
[46] Judges 6:12
[47] Hebrews 10:7

CHAPTER 6

FINANCIAL DISCIPLINE
(HOW TO BEAT "BROKE")

Give me neither poverty nor riches;   -Proverbs 30:8

This chapter will not solve world poverty, nor does it propose to solve the so-called Western "income inequality."[1] Taking money away from a financially disciplined person and "redistributing" it to financially undisciplined people solves nothing and is technically financial malfeasance. Furthermore, in Christ's parable of *The Ten Pieces of Money*, the servant who produced nothing with what he was given was called wicked, and even what he did have was taken from him and given to the servant that had prospered the most.[2] Biblically speaking, poverty is the result of sin, and we will never cure poverty without first curing sin.

This chapter is devoted to helping the willing individual better discipline their finances so that they can begin to dig themselves out of the never-ending cycle of debt, and once debt-free, begin to financially prosper. Not for selfish gain, but so they might be a greater asset to advancing the Gospel of Jesus Christ.

The Bible references money and possessions over 2,000 times, and 11 of the Lord's 39 parables deal with money.[3] These two Bible facts

---

[1] Honestly, as long as you have some people who are better at saving and some people who are better at spending, you will always have income inequality. Furthermore, Jesus Christ said, "the poor you have with you always." See Mark 14:7 and John 12:8.

[2] See Luke 19:12-27. The good and faithful servant prospered by means of diligence and hard work.

[3] The 11 parables are: The Two Debtors (Luke 7:41–43), The Rich Fool (Luke 12:16–21), Parable of the Pearl (Matthew 13:45–46), The Hidden Treasure (Matthew 13:44), Counting the Cost (Luke 14:28–33), The Unforgiving Servant (Matthew 18:23–35), The Lost Coin (Luke 15:8–9), The Unjust Steward (Luke 16:1–13), The Rich Man and Lazarus (Luke 16:19–31), The Workers in the Vineyard (Matthew 20:1–16), The Faithful Servant

alone prove God recognizes that people desperately need wisdom in their financial affairs. Money is a form of power. God meant for money to be a tool, but it usually becomes a god; either an oppressive god called debt or a selfish and cruel god called avarice. Money is also a powerful revealer. It reveals the heart of its possessor. Money reveals who we are, what we want, and what we believe in. We put our money where our heart is. Jesus said, "Where your treasure is, there your heart will be also."[4] Personal money management will also reveal weaknesses in self-control. Consider these recent American financial statistics:

- 78% of American workers live paycheck to paycheck.[5]
- 35% of adults, or 77 million Americans, with a credit file have debt in collections reported in their credit file.[6]
- 70% of Americans don't even have $1,000 in the bank.[7]
- Only 1 in 3 households maintains a budget.[8]
- In 2018, the average American household had $5,700 in credit card debt.[9]
- As reported by Deutsche Bank in 2015, 47% of American households save nothing.

Bible Prosperity And Provision

I must begin by stating that I do believe in prosperity, as I believe every reasonable person does. Every human being strives to prosper in life. That is part of our God-given design. We strive to learn, grow, advance, acquire, influence, and prosper. A good father and husband will strive to provide for his family. Mothers will work their fingers to the bone to provide better

---

(Matthew 24:45–51; Mark 13:34–37; Luke 12:35–48), The Talents or Minas (Matthew 25:14–30; Luke 19:12–27).
   [4] Matthew 6:21
   [5] https://www.cnbc.com/2019/01/09/shutdown-highlights-that-4-in-5-us-workers-live-paycheck-to-paycheck.html
   [6] https://urban.org (accessed August 2019)
   [7] https://money.cnn.com/2016/10/24/pf/financial-mistake-budget/index.html
   [8] Ibid.
   [9] https://www.valuepenguin.com/average-credit-card-debt (accessed August 15, 2019)

for their children. Parents will sacrifice to see their children get a college degree in order to ensure their prosperity and success. To me, this is common sense and praiseworthy. In fact, the New Testament condemns any believer who fails to provide for his own family, even calling them worse than an infidel.[10]

Furthermore, why would I not believe in prosperity? God delights in the prosperity of His servants.[11] God gives His people the power to obtain wealth.[12] Proverbs declares there is profit in all labor.[13] Even the New Testament promises that God will supply all of our needs according to His riches in glory by Christ Jesus.[14] Really, why wouldn't a Christian believe in divine provision and prosperity?

What I do *not* believe in is profligacy, greed, avarice, or excess. I do *not* believe in living so extravagantly that your prosperity becomes a stumbling block for the non-believer or a lightning rod of controversy that maligns the name of Jesus Christ (more on that shortly). I do *not* believe in fairing sumptuously on the tithes and offerings of the widows, single moms, the disenfranchised, and retirees.

I acknowledge that the so-called "prosperity gospel" is laden with perversely misapplied scriptures and hackneyed gimmicks. I also acknowledge that there are many charlatans and hucksters exploiting Christian ignorance and desperation in order to profit themselves.[15] We must understand that there is a huge difference between the preacher that declares the truth that God wants His people to prosper[16] and the fraud who hypes every offering like the Powerball jackpot and declares, "If you want to prosper, you must give to me and get in on this offering!"

---

[10] 1 Timothy 5:8
[11] Psalm 35:27 (NASB)
[12] Deuteronomy 8:18
[13] Proverbs 14:23
[14] Philippians 4:19
[15] Perhaps the only difference between a charlatan and a hireling—you know, the denominational clergy who views his or her role as a "minister" as nothing more than a career in theology—is the amount of money to be made from God's people while not really caring about them. Charlatans tend to be on TV while hirelings tend to be employed as denominational clergy.
[16] See Deuteronomy 8:18 and Psalm 35:27.

The Selfishness Of Extreme Prosperity

There are two main problems that can arise with financial prosperity: 1) it becomes your god, consumes you, and ultimately destroys your life,[17] and/or 2) your wealth becomes a stumbling block or hindrance to the Gospel. Many Christians are familiar with Scripture's direct warnings to not stockpile wealth,[18] to not serve mammon,[19] and to not love money,[20] but few know about the indirect warnings concerning our lifestyle's ability to hinder the Gospel and even blaspheme the name of God. Most God-fearing Christians would agree that the believer should never be a hindrance to the Good News, yet what I dub "extreme prosperity" has become just that—a stumbling block.

We must not forget that our public and private lifestyles are necessary conduits through which the saving message of Christ is both transferred and communicated. Put another way, our lives may be the only epistle some people will ever read. For this reason, the New Testament gives numerous warnings to the believer to take every precaution and never be a stumbling block nor violate the conscience of those who might be observing us. Jesus warned that a drowning death by millstone was preferable when compared to causing a babe to stumble.[21] Paul reiterated the Lord's same concern for Christians to be ever mindful of how we are received and perceived, not using our liberty as an occasion for the flesh.[22]

> [32]**Give none offense, neither to the Jews, nor to the Gentiles, nor to the church of God:** [33]**Even as I please all men in all things, not seeking mine own profit, but the profit of many, that they may be saved.**
> **1 Corinthians 10:32-33**

Paul was sensitive to the conscience of those to whom he was called to minister. He recognized that a reckless or careless lifestyle could

---

[17] See 1 Timothy 6:9-10.
[18] See Matthew 6:19-20.
[19] See Matthew 6:24 and Luke 16:13.
[20] See 1 Timothy 6:10.
[21] See Matthew 18:6; Mark 9:42; Luke 17:2; Acts 24:16; 1 Corinthians 8:12; 10:23-33.
[22] Galatians 5:13

potentially and unintentionally offend the weak conscience of someone, possibly hindering his or her conversion. Paul was so sensitive to this that he never demanded his own rights or privileges. On several occasions he even admitted to purposely rejecting liberties and privileges that were rightfully his simply because they could have hindered the Gospel.[23] Paul even summarized it by saying, I seek not "my own profit, but the profit of many."[24] This is a mature attitude more Christians need to learn. It is immature to demand your own rights in Christ when those rights might be a stumbling block. "Now walkest thou now not charitably . . . Let not your good be evil spoken of."[25]

> **[1]Therefore seeing we have this ministry, as we have received mercy, we faint not; [2]But have renounced the hidden things of dishonesty, not walking in craftiness, nor handling the word of God deceitfully; but by manifestation of the truth commending ourselves to every man's conscience in the sight of God.**
> **2 Corinthians 4:1-2 (emphasis added)**

Too many caught up in the prosperity gospel ignore passages like this. Many smugly defend their hyper-prosperity as a right no one should dare question. Such attitudes reveal a man's real god. But a mature saint will endeavor to commend themself to every man's conscience. If that luxury car, luxury watch, or mansion keeps someone out of heaven, do you really think you deserve it?

Working A Telethon

I once briefly worked a Bible School internship for a Christian television network. Every Tuesday night for about five months, I answered the prayer center phone lines. In case you're not familiar with this concept, I'll explain. Many Christian television programs have a toll-free phone

---

[23] See Acts 20:33-35; 1 Corinthians 9:12; 2 Corinthians 12:13-14; 1 Thess. 2:6-8. It is apparent Paul was not concerned with receiving anything from the churches. He was interested in giving, aiding, and imparting all that he had in order to ensure their success.
[24] 1 Corinthians 10:33
[25] See Romans 14:15b, 16.

number located on the screen that viewers can call for prayer or to make donations. If you were to need prayer, see that phone number, and decide to call, someone like me would answer your call.

There was an understandably strict protocol to follow. I would greet you with the name of the television ministry, followed by my name, maybe ask for your name, then inquire how I might help pray for you. I really enjoyed most of my five months doing this. I was amazed at how open, sincere, and most of all, how desperate people were. I genuinely believe I was able to encourage many dear souls as I prayed with them in their time of need. But then came the month of Telethon Fundraising. Blah!

From what I observed, four or five "big name" ministers were brought in to teach, exhort, and inspire the viewing audience to contribute to the cause of this particular television ministry. This was not just a ministry with a telecast. The ministry for which I was answering phones actually owned television stations and studios all over the world. I recall three guest ministers in particular and their individual fundraising gimmicks (aka deceitful handling of God's Word). I will refer to them as Preacher A, Preacher B, and Preacher C.

Preacher A's message used the story of David and Goliath to motivate the audience to give. The heart of his message was, "Just as David killed Goliath with his own sword, you can't be afraid to kill debt with its own sword." In this case, he was encouraging viewers to use their credit card, the "sword of debt," to go further into debt, that they might kill their personal debt. Sadly, many who were watching that telecast believed the con, not realizing this was manipulative abuse of a powerful story of faith and obedience to God.

Preacher B's time of fundraising happened to fall on or near the Easter/Passover holiday, so he taught on the Passover offering and the blessings of keeping the Passover. In summary, Preacher B did a wonderful job explaining the blessings of God promised to Israel in Exodus 23:14-31. These blessings included angelic protection, God's defense, needs supplied, divine healing, victory, etc. The message was very sound until Preacher B had to twist it to raise money. It was at this point that I remember him saying something like, "Now in order to receive these wonderful promises from God, you need to give a Passover offering." The sermon clearly painted the picture that you had to give in a Passover offering in order to obtain what Jesus had purchased and given to us for free. I just sat and shook my head at the television monitor I was watching from the phone bank. Sadly, many who were watching that telecast believed the con, not realizing that all of those Passover blessings were also New Testament promises because Christ, our Passover, was sacrificed for us.[26]

Preacher C seemed to love scripture address-based offerings, which is where a scripture is taught and then the address of that verse is used as the special dollar amount ascribed to that sermon's offering. For example, if one were to use this gimmick, they might be wise to use Isaiah 61:1-3 as their text and teach on the Spirit of the Lord and the anointing to preach the Gospel. Now when it came time for the offering, $61 could be strongly encouraged as an offering amount. Psalm 1 would not be a wise choice for a reference text since that would only lend itself to a $1 offering,

Preacher C did something just like this and he sealed the deal by saying something like, "Now if you want to get in on the anointing contained in Isaiah 61 you need to sow a $61 offering. I don't know how it works, it just works." Sadly, many who were watching that telecast believed the con, not realizing that Paul taught that every man should give according as he has purposed in his heart, "not reluctantly or in response to pressure."[27]

It broke my heart to sit in the television studio at the phone center, with blowing snow outside, watching the fundraising telecast, not filmed at our location in the snowy Midwest, but shot live in Kauai, Hawaii from a resort overlooking a gorgeous golf course. The hypocrisy and bad optics did not go unnoticed by some in the viewing audience. I had one man call into the hotline and request that I go tell those "idiots" in front of the camera what he thought of them. I kindly informed him that I was not in Kauai, but rather at a television station in the Midwest and that it was currently blowing snow outside. He hung up, but I refused to defend the preachers in Kauai or make an excuse for them.

Another man called in and, without prompting, quickly gave me his name and mailing address. I had to stop him and request an explanation. He kindly started over from the beginning, even spelling his name and mailing address for me this time. I again had to stop him and ask for an

---

[26] 1 Corinthians 5:7b
[27] 2 Corinthians 9:7b NLT

explanation. Realizing I had taken the bait, he stopped and said, "This is my name and address for where you can send the check." I asked, "What check, sir?" At this point he knew the hook was set. He then replied, "The check that's gonna pay off my mortgage, like that charlatan just promised." I remember wryly smiling to myself at his righteous anger and how he had set me up. I politely told him, "Point well taken, sir. And I totally agree with you." To which he hung up.

Perhaps the most grievous conversation I had during that one and only telethon was when Preacher C was requesting his Bible-verse-specific dollar amount offering. I don't remember the text used, but I do remember the amount being somewhere around $50. I answered an incoming phone call from a gentleman in tears. He was going through a very rough season and he wanted to "get in on this limited-time anointing and offering" but he could not possibly afford the $50 offering. He loved the television ministry I was representing and wanted to sponsor it, but he was led to believe it had to be the $50 gimmick offering. He felt like anything less would be an unworthy offering. The whole scenario angered me. On the phone was a sincere brother in Christ grasping at straws; on the telecast was the stereotypical televangelist: gold-chained, hair-dyed, pompadoured, smooth-talking huckster, suckering and swindling God's people out of money they didn't have.

Without running down the polished swindler, I took the liberty to teach the precious brother on the phone what the Bible says about offerings. I mentioned Paul's teaching about giving as you purposed in your heart. I encouraged him that God only required obedience and cheerfulness in his offering. In the end, that man pledged $5 a month to a ministry he loved and trusted. As for me, I vowed never to be a gimmick preacher, charlatan, or prosperity preacher, and I vowed in my heart to never view or teach money in an offensive and Gospel-hindering way.

Yes, God wants to provide for us, even prosper us. Yes, God wants us flourishing, abounding, and able to care for others; but if the last 30 years of American Christian ministry has taught us anything, it should have taught us that there comes a point where people are offended by extreme prosperity. People can be turned off to God by a preacher's excessiveness, extravagance, and opulence. And to be perfectly honest, only the preacher is getting rich off of these gimmick offerings. When will enough be enough?

Balanced Prosperity

For hundreds of years, the West has enjoyed the highest standard of living in the world. Why? Because the West developed under the Judeo-Christian culture—a culture that innovates, creates, invents, develops, educates, and prospers. The resulting prosperity created the high standard of living that has defined the Western world ever since. Simply put, everywhere Christianity has gone, prosperity followed. Consider the words of Charles Darwin as observed by W.E. Biedersolf:

> *What did Darwin mean when he said, "A man about to be shipwrecked on some unknown coast will devoutly pray that the lesson of the missionary will have reached that far"? He meant that where the Gospel has not gone civilization has not gone, and such a shipwrecked man would likely find himself in the soup tureen of husky cannibals.*[28]

Consider the simple fact that every country considered third world or a developing nation has paganism at the core of its culture. Muslim countries would have no wealth were it not for their oil supplies—oil needed and purchased by the West—the same West that also developed the combustion engine, cars, and the Industrial Revolution. The poorest countries in the world still worship the demons of their forefathers. Countries like Haiti are currently humanitarian money pits because of their rejection of the Gospel and commitment to demon worship. As Benjamin Disraeli, one of Britain's great prime ministers from the 19th Century said, "All countries that reject the cross wilt . . ."[29]

On the other hand, America, the wealthiest, most innovative nation ever known in the history of mankind, also happens to be the only nation founded upon the Bible in order to worship the God of the Bible.

---

[28] Quoted in D. James Kennedy, *What if the Bible Had Never Been Written* (Nashville, Thomas Nelson, Inc. Publishers, 1998), 42.
[29] Benjamin Disraeli, *Beaconsfield's Life of Lord Bentinck*, quoted in Lawson, *Greatest Thoughts About Jesus Christ*, 131.

Coincidence? The Gospel brings the presence of God everywhere it goes, and His presence brings innovation, life, provision, and . . . prosperity.

Prosperity Is Relative

All prosperity is relative. On my many trips to the foreign mission field, I have become ever mindful that prosperity is a relative term. If you don't believe God wants you to prosper financially, you have probably never traveled to a developing nation or, if you have, you failed to notice how prosperous you really are (especially as a Westerner).

As of this publication,[30] the average Ugandan[31] earns approximately $100 a month. (And I might add that Uganda is currently prospering better than many African nations.) That is an annual income of $1,200. According to 2015 U.S. Census Bureau data, the median household American income is $56,516. So in evaluating the relativity of prosperity, let us consider some typical non-luxury American purchases and how they measure up to the average Ugandan's income. My $35 *Timex Ironman* watch is nearly a third of a Ugandan's monthly income. The $100 trail shoes I might wear while walking around the streets of Kampala or on the ferry crossing the Nile would cost a Ugandan one-month's income. The $200 suit I might preach in while in Uganda is worth two months' salary, as is the $200 suitcase I frequently travel with.  The iPhone I travel with in order to FaceTime home and record video or take pictures is worth 10 months' salary. The typical $2,500 airline ticket it takes to fly me to Uganda and home again is equal to two years' income. My Toyota truck was approximately $24,000 brand new. That's worth 20 years' income to the average Ugandan. And what about my modest home? More money than the average Ugandan might see in several lifetimes. Even the laptop I'm using to write this book is more than a year's salary to a Ugandan.

Honestly, the $100 per month the average Ugandan might earn would barely cover the typical American's monthly cellphone bill. Or what about the $500 most American households spend on a game console? Or what about that Disney vacation the average American family of four might

---

[30] First printing 2019.
[31] I chose Uganda because our church has been very active there.

take? You may by no means be rich, but compared to 98% of the world, you probably live like a king.

Perhaps I should adjust my semantic and say, "I unabashedly believe in God's divine provision." I believe that serving Jesus Christ gives Christians an advantage that the world does not have. I believe His promises of provision, favor, blessing, and witty inventions are designed to propel us forward in life, draw people to us, and must be used to finance the Gospel.[32] I also believe that these promises work in the bush of Africa, the tundra of Siberia, and in the slums of India. Why? Because they are God's promises and they are not dependent upon natural economies.

It must also be noted that when the King James Bible speaks of "prospering" or "to prosper and be in health," both the Hebrew and Greek words translated "prosper" are not limited only to *money*. The definition for biblical prosperity includes: *good success, make progress, advancement,* and *to be profitable.* 3 John 2 is the oft-quoted scripture concerning prosperity. Remember from the previous chapter, the word for prosperity literally means *the good road.*[33]

Bible Basics

We should begin with some very simple biblical principles. Chief among those is the fact that the Bible never speaks positively of poverty.[34] Jesus praised the poor in spirit (also known as humility), but He never lauded poverty as a beatific state.[35] This is not to say that earthly riches are God's endorsement. Remember, the rich man went to hell while Lazarus went to Abraham's bosom, and the church at Smyrna was highly regarded by Jesus Christ though it was in deep tribulation and poverty.[36]

God is not against His people having money. He's just against money having His people. But the Bible does more than tell us that God wants to prosper His people and bring success. The Bible puts the greater

---

[32] 1 Corinthians 16:2
[33] Romans 1:10
[34] Proverbs 10:15; 13:18; 20:13; 23:21
[35] The Beatitudes of Matthew 5 derive their name from the Latin *beatitude*, meaning, "perfect happiness."
[36] See Revelation 2:8-10.

emphasis on how we are to view and handle money. While the prosperity gospel has evolved into nothing but a manifestation of greed, avarice, and materialism, the doctrine of divine provision includes wealth, heart motive, and personal fiscal responsibility.

Wealth is a powerful tool. In the hands of a skilled artisan, tools can be used to build, repair, and create. In the hands of an inexperienced or reckless fool, the same tool can vandalize, tear down, or even maim. God wants His people to possess both the skill and the maturity necessary to safely handle wealth. We *must* know how to handle money and material goods.

The Painful Truth About Prodigality

Luke 15 records what may be considered the most famous Gospel parable—*The Parable of the Prodigal Son*. Even the secular world understands the concept of "the prodigal son returning home." To be clear, the Bible never refers to the wayward son as "the prodigal," or even as "a prodigal." Theologians, Bible footnotes, and preachers have carried on the accurate tradition of calling the young man in this particular parable the prodigal son.[37]

In the parable, a wealthy man's younger son requests that his father grant an early distribution of his share of the inheritance. The father honors the younger son's request, even giving the eldest son his portion as well. Soon after, the younger son leaves home and begins to waste his inheritance on "foolish living."[38] In a cruel twist of fate, just as soon as he runs out of money, a great famine arises, ultimately bringing about his famous repentance and return home. It is a tremendous parable about sin, repentance, and restoration. However, I find it carries with it a very common modern misunderstanding. Most Christians don't know what a prodigal really is.

Many people understand a prodigal to be someone who leaves home to go and live a debaucherous life for a season, only to grow disgusted at their own sin, eventually repent, return home again, and find forgiveness. Although this is certainly a wonderful summary of the story presented in

---

[37] The first usage of "the prodigal son" dates to approximately 1550 AD.
[38] Luke 15:13 (CSB)

this parable, this is not what a prodigal does. If this definition were accurate, many Christians could argue they have never been a prodigal, because they have never lived a life of purposed debauchery. But as it stands, once we understand the true definition of prodigality, and once we are enlightened to some of the subtle phrases in this parable, the painful truth is: almost every Christian has been or is currently a prodigal.

Look up *prodigal* in any dictionary and the definition will read something akin to: *wastefully extravagant, profuse, spending freely, spending in excess.* What is a prodigal? A prodigal is someone who wastes money or resources, often recklessly so. Have you ever been guilty of wasting resources? Sure you have. Consider what Luke 15 says about the younger brother (emphasis is mine):

> [13]"**And not many days after, the younger son gathered all together, journeyed to a far country, and there wasted his possessions with prodigal[39] living. **[14]**But when he had spent all**, there arose a severe famine in that land, and he began to be in want."** Luke 15:13-14 (NKJV)

So why is this parable called *The Parable of the Prodigal Son*? Because the younger son took his father's substance and wasted it on excessive and foolish lifestyles. This inheritance was supposed to last the son the rest of his life, but he managed to squander it all in a matter of weeks.

Later in the parable, the older brother accuses him of wasting the inheritance on prostitutes, but it should be pointed out that the parable itself does not make that accusation. Besides, how did the older brother know he wasted the money on harlots? The prodigality occurred in a far country. Did the older brother follow him there or send spies out after him?

The point is: the parable is historically called *The Prodigal Son* because he wastes his father's resources. On what—it does not necessarily matter. The wealth is misused and squandered. And we've all done it. We have all been given resources by God through our jobs, pensions, retirement funds, investments, etc., only to waste it foolishly.

---

[39] The Greek word here is *asōtōs* and is rendered *riotous, prodigal, foolish, wild, reckless,* and *loose lifestyle* in different Bible translations.

Churches have wasted the tithe on frivolous social fads. Ministers have wasted the offering on unnecessarily lavish expenditures and purchases. Laity wastes money on everything from trying to keep up with the Joneses to just eating out too much. Most prodigality can be prevented with a simple budget.

This brings us to the subject of budgets. Though not as glorious or spectacular as miracle-debt-cancellation-offerings or the mysterious great uncle's inheritance, a budget is by far a more proven, more biblical, and infinitely more dependable method than either of the above. If you have a pulse, the wisdom of God demands a budget. In fact, it will be impossible for any person, family, business, or ministry to prosper without a budget.

Your Desperate Need For A Budget

The absolute best way to discipline one's financial appetite is to develop and live according to a budget. There are no "get-out-of-debt" quick options, no matter what Christian television fundraisers proclaim. Those kinds of financial gimmicks only appeal to people who are bad with money to begin with, so to them, it is just another risky venture not unlike a lotto ticket.

The truth is, you didn't get into debt overnight and you're not going to get out of debt overnight. Sure, God could deliver you from your debtors by some supernatural means, but why would He? You wouldn't learn anything about financial stewardship if He were always bailing you out. God is not an enabler of financial malfeasance. But, on the other hand, if God walks you out of debt by means of His wisdom and your self-discipline, well . . . the long road back to solvency or even surplus would serve as a great deterrent to never go back down the road of wasteful spending. The *looong* road out of debt is paved by consistent, self-controlled obedience to a budget. And guess what? The Bible is full of budgets.

The Tithe

The tithe, meaning *the tenth part*, is itself a standing budget. By implication, the tithe is the first budget established in the Bible. In order for Abraham to institute the first tithe as an act of worship, he had to first know how many cows, camels, sheep, gold, garments, bolts of fabric, swords, helmets, spears, pounds of oil, jars of figs, etc., he had from the spoils of war before he could accurately give 10% to Melchizedek.[40]

The commandment and spiritual law called the tithe is a budget demanding to be obeyed. If God requires a tenth part of all increase, then all increase must be accounted for and the tenth part separated and given to God. When obeyed, this divine budget promises to rebuke the devourer (loss) and open up the windows of heaven (gain).[41] According to Malachi 3:10, the tenth is to be taken to God's "storehouse" in order for there to be provision there. This sounds like a type of savings account that benefits the House of God and those in need of its ministry. It will be impossible for a Christian to prosper without tithing and budgeting.

Joseph's Divine Budget

Genesis 41 records how the Pharaoh of Joseph's day had two dreams neither he nor any of the magicians or wise men could interpret. These dreams greatly troubled him. Joseph proved to be the only man who could explain to Pharaoh the meaning. If you recall, the first dream involved seven fat cows being consumed by seven skinny cows. The second dream involved seven thin heads of grain swallowing up seven healthy heads of grain.

The two dreams were a prophetic warning concerning seven years of prosperity followed by seven dire years of famine. As Joseph explained, "The reason the dream was given to Pharaoh in two forms is that the matter has been firmly decided by God, and God will do it soon."[42] But it seems that Joseph wasn't just anointed to interpret the two dreams; he was also anointed to give Pharaoh the godly counsel necessary to beat the impending divine dearth. Consider Joseph's prophetic counsel:

> [33] **And now let Pharaoh look for a discerning and wise man and put him in charge of the land of Egypt. [34]Let**

---

[40] See Genesis 14:17-24 and Hebrews 7:1-9.
[41] See Malachi 3:10-11.
[42] Genesis 41:32 (NIV)

> **Pharaoh appoint commissioners over the land to take a fifth of the harvest of Egypt during the seven years of abundance. ³⁵They should collect all the food of these good years that are coming and store up the grain under the authority of Pharaoh, to be kept in the cities for food. ³⁶This food should be held in reserve for the country, to be used during the seven years of famine that will come upon Egypt, so that the country may not be ruined by the famine.** **Genesis 41:33-36 (NIV)**

This plan seemed good to Pharaoh and all his officials. Joseph was set over this work and made second in command of Egypt. Joseph's solution was basically a budget that emphasized a savings plan—a 20% savings plan. (I wish the U.S. Government believed in such budgetary plans.) As I study Joseph's plan, a simple pattern emerges capable of financially prospering any person, household, ministry, business, school, or government.

- Verse 33—**Step 1**: Someone must be in charge of the budget, preferably the wisest and most discerning person involved. If you're a single person . . . don't fail yourself.
- Verse 34—**Step 2**: Build your financial budget.[43] Joseph mandated 20% savings on every harvest for seven years. Determine how much you will save and invest after you've paid your tithe, given your offerings, and paid your bills.
- Verse 35—**Step 3**: The budget produces a surplus called savings. Savings should be greater when the surplus is greater. The savings are earmarked. In Joseph's case, the savings were earmarked for food. Your savings may be earmarked for a new home, college tuition, Christmas spending, etc. Save with a purpose in mind and set a goal.

---

[43] The hands-on mechanics of "how to build a budget" are beyond the scope of this book. Countless books and websites are available to aid in this area should the reader require further assistance.

- Verse 36—**Step 4**: The savings are set aside in reserve and are to remain untouched except for their intended purpose. Joseph commanded the harvest savings to remain untouched until the seven years of famine hit.

Here again are the four elements to Joseph's divine budget: 1) someone is in charge; 2) build a budget that includes savings; 3) the savings are earmarked and untouched; 4) the savings are used for their intended purpose at the appointed time. I find this plan to be remarkably simple, yet this was God's supernatural plan to prosper Egypt.

As with all budgets, the Joseph Plan (as we shall call it) required discipline. Apparently, Egypt was incredibly fruitful for the first 7 years in order for a total sum of 1.4 years[44] worth of produce to feed Egypt and the known world for 7 years of famine. The Joseph Plan did not permit unnecessary consumption. Twenty percent was demanded from every crop. One in five bushels of grain was stockpiled. One in five bushels of beans was stockpiled. It would have been easy for the Egyptians to expand their consumption during those plenteous years just as many people expand their standard of living every time they get a raise, but the strictness of Joseph's budget prevented such gluttonous prodigality. A budget (of any kind) is a tremendous aid in exercising self-control.

In the end, Joseph's budget brought a two-fold blessing upon Egypt: 1) thanks to their food savings, Egypt was able to maintain its independence in time of famine; 2) the discipline of Joseph's strict seven-year budget allowed Egypt to actually prosper in time of dearth by selling what they had stockpiled. Rather than Egypt having to go to the surrounding nations for help, the surrounding nations came to Egypt to buy bread. Thanks to a budget, the famine actually prospered Egypt. Budgets aid wealth production.

Moses' Tabernacle Budget

Moses had a budget for the building of the Tabernacle. Moses received a blueprint for the Tabernacle from God upon Mount Sinai. A blueprint is

---

[44] (7 years) x (20%) = 1.40 years worth of savings during the prosperous years.

a type of building budget. He knew exactly what was needed for the building of the Tabernacle. This included gold, silver, brass, linen of blue, purple, scarlet, fine linen, goats' hair, rams' skin, shittim wood, oil, spices, gemstones.[45]

> [5]And they spake unto Moses, saying, The people bring much more than enough for the service of the work, which the LORD commanded to make. [7]For the stuff they had was sufficient for all the work to make it, and too much.
> **Exodus 36:5, 7**

Moses' building budget let his helpers know when they had enough resources for the task at hand. Too many Christians don't know what they have need of, so they don't know when they have enough, or worse yet, they don't know what to ask for in prayer. Many Christians wisely pray, "my God shall supply all of my needs according to His riches in glory by Christ Jesus,"[46] but without a budget, how will you know just exactly what those needs are?

David's Budget

David had a budget for Solomon's Temple. David received the blueprint for Solomon's Temple from the Spirit of God. He then began to prepare for the Temple's construction based on the blueprint's[47] demands. This blueprint was a type of budget. It would have shown what was needed to build it the way God wanted it. Without this building budget, no one would have known what or how much to provide. David spent years stockpiling and preparing gold, silver, brass, iron, wood, cedar, gemstones, and hewn stone. David saw what was needed to accomplish something, and he began to budget for it. The cost of the Temple was exponential, and David had to save for years in order to meet the budget.[48] May God's modern people learn how to save for years in order to accomplish greater things for Him.

---

[45] See Exodus 25:1-9.
[46] Philippians 4:19
[47] See 1 Chronicles 28:11-19 (NASB).
[48] See 1 Chronicles 22:1-5; 28:14-19; 29:2-5.

Solomon's Kingdom Budget

Solomon had a treasurer and a secretary for his kingdom. Ahishar managed the household, which would have included finances and personnel, and Adoniram was over the kingdom's taxes and levies. Solomon had to know his kingdom's needs and then levy taxes to supply those needs. He was the wisest man ever, and yet he had to have a budget to run his home and his kingdom.[49] The result of Solomon's reign—a reign successful due in part to his use of budgets—is declared in 1 Kings 4:25, "And Judah and Israel dwelt safely, every man under his vine and under his fig tree, from Dan to Beersheba, all the days of Solomon." This verse is very profound for two reasons. First, the phrase "every man under his own vine and under his fig tree" depicts a scene of peace and prosperity.[50] Second, the phrase "from Dan to Beersheba" is a common Hebraism used to describe the entirety of the Israelite nation. It is the equivalent of Americans saying "from sea to sea" or "from coast to coast." Together, these two phrases paint the picture that, due in part to Solomon's wise use of budgets, all of Israel from sea to sea (so to speak) dwelt safely and securely, each person having their own fig trees, vines, and personal prosperity. That is the power and blessing of budgets!

Solomon's Daily Food Budget

Solomon's household was substantial. As king, it fell to Solomon to provide food for the massive household and staff on a daily basis. The administration of its daily maintenance was a colossal undertaking, requiring 12 officers to oversee.[51] The Wisdom of Solomon solved this daunting task with a budget—a food budget. Budgets reveal two critical things: what you need and when you need it; and Solomon's food budget was no exception. He calculated the daily needs of his household, down to the number of lambs per meal.[52] His daily menu included: 185 bushels of fine flour, 375 bushels of meal, 10 fat oxen, 20 oxen from the pasture, 100 sheep, deer, gazelles, roebucks, and choice fowls. Each of

---

[49] See 1 Kings 4:1-6.
[50] See also Micah 4:4 and Zechariah 3:10.
[51] 1 Kings 4:7
[52] See 1 Kings 4:22-23.

the 12 officers knew what was needed and when it was needed, for each of them delivered the necessary provision in the month assigned to them. Can you imagine being one of those 12 officers? Your entire career under Solomon was spent organizing and collecting the foodstuffs necessary for your allotted month. And just as soon as you had delivered your monthly supply, you would have had to quickly refocus your efforts on collecting your next assigned month's supply (which would not have been due for another year). A prosperous nation employs many people, or to state it biblically, "Righteousness exalteth a nation."[53]

Nehemiah's Daily Food Budget

Following in the footsteps of King Solomon nearly 900 years earlier, Nehemiah, King Artaxerxes' newly appointed governor over the Persian territory of Judea, also had a daily food allowance. This food budget took into consideration how many people were eating daily at the governor's table. In this case, it was 150 Jews and rulers and an unspecified number of heathen who had gathered to help Nehemiah.[54] The book of Nehemiah records the daily food budget as one ox, six choice sheep, some poultry, and a generous supply of wine every ten days.

Jesus' Budget

Jesus had an accountant for his ministry. Judas managed the Lord's ministerial finances.[55] Many people supported Jesus' ministry and He had to have someone budget and manage those finances.[56] Jesus was always giving to the poor and was prone to feeding his disciples.[57] Judas kept the budget, but he also robbed the budget. Are you a financial Judas?

Budgets Reveal Needs

Philippians 4 contains one of the greatest Bible promises concerning material needs. After a nine-verse exhortation on offerings,

---

[53] Proverbs 14:34
[54] See Nehemiah 5:14-19.
[55] John 12:6
[56] Luke 8:3
[57] See Mark 6:37; Luke 9:13; and John 12:5; 13:29.

ministerial support, contentment, hunger vs. satiation, and prosperity vs. privation, Paul concludes in verse 19 by saying, "But my God shall supply all your need according to His riches in glory by Christ Jesus." God wants to supply our needs! God wants to take care of us. He revealed Himself to Abraham as *Jehovah Jireh*—The LORD who supplies. When Abraham needed a sacrifice, God supplied him with one. This verse is a wonderful Bible promise to pray when needs arise.

Elizabeth Elliot is quoted saying, "God has promised to supply all our needs. What we don't have now, we don't need now." Such a quote encourages us to trust God when times are tough and supply seems meager. But how do we determine what we need? Why, with a budget, of course.

Growing up, my dad would often drill into me the difference between *needs* and *wants*. It seems like I always had way more *wants* than I had *needs*, but that's probably how it is with most children. Sometimes adults also have trouble distinguishing between their needs and their wants. Christians need to understand the difference if they want to properly apply Philippians 4:19 in prayer. God promised to always supply every *need*, not every *want*. He promised to supply our daily bread, and He only provides the amount of bread we need today.

Daily, Convenient, And Pleasant Bread

Bread makes for a wonderful topical Bible study. Not including Jesus as the Bread of Life,[58] the Bible speaks of three types of bread: *Daily Bread*, *Convenient Bread*, and *Pleasant Bread*. Bread represents God's daily provision in our life.

The concept of *daily bread* is first presented as manna during the Exodus. Coming out of Egypt, Israel did not need money every day as we do—they needed food. Manna was the divine provision God sent as an answer to Israel's complaints and comparisons to Egypt, where, though they were slaves, they did "eat bread to the full."[59] And though it was a

---

[58] Jesus is, of course, the Bread of Life that comes down from heaven. He was foreshadowed in the daily manna from heaven—also called "bread to the full" in Exodus 16:8.

[59] More accurately, manna was God's answer to Israel's third of ten temptations of God.

demonstration of God's ability to easily provide the daily needs of His people, He also used the manna as a test to see if they would walk in His ways or not. Yes, God would supply their daily needs, but would they obey Him in the daily appropriation of the manna?

It was the Israelites responsibility to go out and collect the manna according to a "certain rate."[60] The certain rate, or daily ration, was prescribed by God as an omer per person per day.[61] This implies that supernatural provision does not negate the personal responsibility of the work necessary to obtain it nor does it exclude budgetary considerations necessary to manage it. (Put another way: God sends the supply, but it must be collected and budgeted.) In the case of manna, everybody collected the exact same amount. This may have been done to create a sense of equality in the newly liberated nation.

For six days the Israelites would awake to find more than enough manna lying around everywhere. We know that some gathered more (perhaps out of greed or fear) and others gathered less (perhaps out of insecurity or a poverty mindset). Either way, he that gathered abundantly had nothing left over and he that gathered little lacked nothing. Each had enough for their daily needs. On the sixth day they were commanded to gather twice as much in preparation for the Sabbath, indicating God expects His people to be able to practice the self-restraint necessary to establish savings. Some obeyed the sixth day double-portion command. Others did not and God was angered. If we apply this principle to *our* daily needs being supplied, we can see that God rejoices to supply our needs, but He will inspect us to see if we are obedient to Him with that daily supply.

The Lord taught us to request daily bread as part of the Lord's Prayer, "give us this day, our daily bread (our daily needs supplied)." This further confirms the symbolism that *daily bread* represents God's ability to supply our daily needs, whether it is literal bread, water, eggs, fuel, equipment, or money. We may be allowed to prove God with the tithe,[62] but He proves us with our stewardship of His daily supply. Daily

---

[60] See Exodus 16:4, also translated as "a day's portion" (RSV). Thus, "give us this day our daily bread."
[61] Exodus 16:16; approximately 2 to 3.5 liters in volume or 3.5 lbs. (1.6 kg.) in weight.
[62] Malachi 3:10

bread is just enough to get you to the next day. If we don't have it today, we don't need it today. If we need it today and we don't have it today, it may be that He provided it yesterday and we already ate it.

Convenient Bread

Convenient bread is a King James term found in Proverbs 30:8-9:

> **⁸Remove far from me vanity and lies: give me neither poverty nor riches; feed me with <u>food [bread] convenient for me</u>: ⁹Lest I be full, and deny thee, and say, Who is the LORD? or lest I be poor, and steal, and take the name of my God in vain.**

Convenient bread is bread that God has prescribed or ordained for you. This is bread that is according to the God-ordained boundaries in your life.[63] God has set different boundaries in every person's life. College students have different boundaries and responsibilities than do entrepreneurs. Pastors have different boundaries than do retirees in the nursing home.

If my daily walk of obedience to God requires six loaves of bread, God is obligated to supply six loaves because He promised to supply my needs. If my life of obedience to God only requires two loaves of bread each day, wisdom dictates that I remain faithful over those two loaves and do not covet the man who requires six loaves.

Feeding on the sin of covetousness, socialism wants to take two loaves away from the man with six loaves and give them to the guy with only two, so that everyone has four loaves and all things are equal (not fair, not just—just equal). This is famously called *equality of outcome* and is done with total disregard for the different boundaries God has set on the two-loaf man versus the six-loaf man. Socialism may sound pleasant when you're lazy, greedy, or have a secular worldview, but it is really nothing more than man's wisdom mocking God for the sake of being "equal." We

---

[63] Hebrew *(choq): ordinance, prescribed portion, specific decree, limit or boundary.*

must understand God is not a God of equality.[64] He *is* a God of justice and impartiality, and while He does promise *equality of opportunity* (e.g. "whosoever will"), He has never promised equality of outcome.

Contrary to many progressive, humanistic, political ideologies (like socialism), mankind is not a homogenously equal community. The only thing equal in the Kingdom of God[65] is our value to Him. God paid the same price for every person—the blood of Jesus Christ. We are all valued the same, but we are not all equal.[66] This is by God's design. We are each created by God with different graces, callings, abilities, talents, assignments, boundaries, and different stations[67] in life. We each develop differently, and therefore, require a different supply. The existence of a modern wealth disparity is due in part to the concept of *convenient bread* and is only exacerbated by systemic shiftlessness.

According to Proverbs 30:8, *convenient bread* is neither poverty nor riches. It is more than just the *daily bread* I need to exist. It is just the amount of supply I require to do what God has called me to do. It is the promise of the divine supply for my station and assignment in life. If there is not enough, I might be tempted to steal. If there is too much, I might be tempted to walk away from God. *Convenient bread* is not one omer per person per day. It echoes Philippians 4:19: "And my God shall supply all of your need according to His riches in glory by Christ Jesus." Each person has a different need because we are all different and individual by the design of God.

Pleasant Bread

Pleasant bread is mentioned in Daniel 10:3 as Daniel fasted to seek the Lord. This phrase can also be translated *desirable bread*, *tasty food*, or

---

[64] There is a big difference between equality and equity. Equality means all things equal. Equity means just and fair. God is a God of equity, not equality.

[65] Not even eternal judgment will be equal, neither rewards nor punishments. See Luke 10:10-16; 12:48 for punishment disparities. See Luke 19:12-27; 1 Corinthians 3:12-15 for reward disparities.

[66] Consider also the Body of Christ, each member is different with a different role to play and different supply requirements. See 1 Corinthians 12:12-21.

[67] By "station in life," we mean the position of life in which a person has been assigned to stand or remain, but it is a position that serves a purpose. It can be reflected in social standing.

rich food. At this time (the third year of King Cyrus' reign over Persia), Daniel was a high-ranking officer under Cyrus and was known by his Babylonian name Belteshazzar.[68] As a man of high authority, Daniel would have been afforded great wealth, prestige, and means. That Persian governors ate better than everyone else should not surprise us. In fact, this notion is supported by Nehemiah's admission of rejecting "the bread of the governor."[69] Since Daniel was of such high rank in the Persian kingdom, He would have also been allotted food of a much higher caliber.[70]

Pleasant bread (aka "the governor's bread" or "the king's bread") represents the materialism those of high society can easily obtain. This represents a daily provision that God has not appointed or promised to all people. When Daniel became a man in high authority, *pleasant bread* was afforded him as a benefit of his office. He came by it easily and honestly. He did not have to obsess over acquiring it. He was not consumed of *pleasant bread*. As Hebrews 13:5 commands, "be content with such things as ye have: for he hath said, I will never leave thee, nor forsake thee."

Pleasant bread is more than *convenient bread* and far beyond the promise of *daily bread*. Proverbs 23:1-3 warns of lusting after *pleasant bread*:

> **¹When thou sittest to eat with a ruler, consider diligently what is before thee: ²And put a knife to thy throat, if thou be a man given to appetite. ³Be not desirous of his dainties (pleasant bread): for they are deceitful meat (bread).**[71]

---

[68] See Daniel 1:7; 2:26; and 4:8. *Belteshazzar* means, "may he protect the life of the king;" a fitting name for such a favored and trusted servant. He was given this name in order to disassociate him from his God and to naturalize him into Babylonian culture.

[69] Nehemiah 5:14-15

[70] Daniel rejected the same dainty meats (a daily provision of the king's meat) when he was first taken into the king's school of eunuchs. No doubt Daniel suspected the king's food had probably been offered to pagan deities first. See Daniel 1:3-8.

[71] Hebrew (*lechem*): same as bread in Exodus 16:4 and "food" in Proverbs 30:8-9.

Here we see the same principle of *convenient bread* versus *pleasant bread*. The proverb assumes that the reader is of a normal station in life, accustomed to living on the promise of *daily bread* and *convenient bread*. But the proverb offers a warning should the reader ever be given the opportunity to fellowship with someone from a higher station in life. Watch out! Judge yourself! Don't fall in love with what the ruler is accustomed to. It is deceitful. Everything that glitters ain't always gold.

Proverbs continues to offer wisdom in this scenario by transitioning from a warning about food to a warning about money. Proverbs 23 continues:

> **[4]Do not weary yourself to gain wealth, Cease from your consideration of it. [5]When you set your eyes on it, it is gone. For wealth certainly makes itself wings like an eagle that flies toward the heavens. (NASB)**

It is interesting to note that Solomon transitions from a caution concerning fancy food to a warning about money, but really the two are inseparable. To sit and observe a man's pleasant bread is to understand the amount of money it represents. It would be akin to sitting at a red light and looking over and seeing a Ferrari next to you. You would instantly understand what kind of money such a car represents. The next obvious thought might be, "I wonder what they do for a living?" Most people would go no further than that in their mind because they understand that such *pleasant bread* is not their lot in life, and they are perfectly content with what they have been given. In short, they have no appetite for expensive Italian sports cars. But for some, observing a Ferrari from the seat of their well-used minivan might awaken a whole host of emotions and appetites from insecurity and minivan shame, to daydreams of driving their dream car and mortgaging their home to get one. For the ultra-rich, a Ferrari is a hobby. For the middle class, a Ferrari is a dangerous obsession.

The point is most people have a secret materialistic appetite that usually lies dormant just as long as it is not awakened. Too often though, Christians hurt themselves financially by not reining in their materialism and by spending money they don't have to try to eat the king's *pleasant bread* every day. The key is to recognize the station of life where God has currently assigned us and live there with contentment and faithfulness.

We are not all called to live in the king's palace. We are not all called to live in mansions, drive luxury cars, or have a toy for every expensive hobby. May God bless us and see fit to promote us, but we cannot despise the day of small beginnings. We must serve God where we are found today.[72]

Coming back to Daniel, he did not seek after the king's *pleasant bread*; he sought God and God saw fit to elevate him to a place in life where *pleasant bread* was normal. Contrary to what decades of horrific prosperity teaching have taught, we are not promised the king's bread; rather we have been commanded to be content.

> **[6]But godliness with contentment is great gain. [7]For we brought nothing into this world, and it is certain we can carry nothing out. [8]And having food and raiment let us be therewith content.**   **1 Timothy 6:6-8**

Here Paul echoes the two points of Christ's exhortation in Matthew 6:24-34: food and clothes. If God can feed birds and clothe lilies, He can certainly provide for the believer who seeks the Kingdom first.

Fallacy arises when we assume everyone will be rich. The Bible never promises that everyone will be rich any more than it promises that everyone will live in kings' houses.[73] Jesus revealed we would always have poor people in society.[74] Besides, as previously covered, prosperity is relative. Even the poorest American has greater material wealth than most people in developing nations.

God's Kingdom has always included the rich, the poor, and everyone in between. Beginning in Exodus 30:15, God commanded both rich and poor to give the same offering for the care and maintenance of

---

[72] See 1 Corinthians 7:20-24 (NASB).

[73] See Matthew 11:8. John the Baptist is exalted as the greatest of Old Testament prophets (Matt. 11:11) and still his calling never saw him elevated to great riches. The only time he saw the inside of a king's house was when his head was on a platter.

[74] See Matthew 26:11; Mark 14:7; and John 12:8.

the Tabernacle—half a shekel. Proverbs 22:2 states that the rich and poor have a common bond, the Lord is the maker of them both (NASB). David observed in Psalm 49:1-2 that the world is inhabited by both low and high, rich and poor. In fact, the New Testament recognizes that there are brethren of humble circumstances and there are also rich brethren.[75] And even at the end of time, in Babylon, there will still be rich, poor, and everyone in between.[76] In order to be wise stewards of our daily supply, we must recognize where God has set us in life. Knowing our station in life will also aid us in resisting the king's dainties.

Please don't misunderstand me, God can and does promote people upward through the echelons of society and life, but those are His prerogatives. We must believe in the increases of God. God is the judge; He puts down one and exalts another.[77] Hannah prophesied such promotions in 1 Samuel 2:7-8 (NASB):

> **[7]The LORD makes poor and rich; He brings low, He also exalts. [8]He raises the poor from the dust, He lifts the needy from the ash heap To make them sit with nobles, And inherit a seat of honor; For the pillars of the earth are the LORD's And He set the world on them.**

God can cause even the lowest person of the humblest station of life to sit at the king's table,[78] but that does not happen for everyone. We must recognize our station in life and thrive where God has us today.[79] Only He knows what He has planned for us in the future.

---

[75] James 1:9-10 (NASB)

[76] Revelation 13:16

[77] Psalm 75:6-7

[78] I recommend the autobiography of Booker T. Washington, *Up from Slavery*. Mr. Washington was born into slavery nine years before the Emancipation Proclamation. His faith in Jesus Christ and impeccable character caused his life to arise from the chaos of the Reconstruction. He was the first black man to dine in the White House (as a guest of President Theodore Roosevelt) and he became an adviser to other presidents.

[79] For a hard passage, see 1 Corinthians 7:20-24 (NASB). Here Paul encourages believers to remain in their station or calling wherein they were called, even slavery, unless they can become free and advance upward. In which case the Gospel compels you to do so. Also, regressing backward in life by selling yourself into slavery is forbidden.

Balanced Bread:
Satisfaction vs. Contentment

I would be remiss if I did not address the biblical tension I have inadvertently presented thus far. That is, I don't want anyone to come through this chapter thinking they should not aspire to advance in life. Like most biblical doctrines, there are tensions that must be relieved and ditches that must be avoided. Prosperity and provision present us with such dilemmas. Thus far, I have covered prosperity from the perspective of having a budget and recognizing your station in life. I will now flip the perspective around and, in an effort to deconstruct the poverty mindset, encourage the reader to aspire to higher levels of influence, provision, wealth, and promotion; for God is a God of increase.[80]

The Bible presents us with two different philosophies for viewing life: *satisfaction* and *contentment*. These words are typically used interchangeably, but the Bible makes a clear distinction between the two. To be *satisfied* means you have had your fill and you desire nothing else. Another definition states *to put to an end by sufficient or ample provision*. Either way, if you are satisfied, you have no intention of advancing any further than your current position. The attitude of satisfaction can be so strong that even if God were to call you higher in life, you would refuse Him because you have decided what you possess is sufficient.

Genesis 25:8 reveals that Abraham died *after* he was "satisfied and satiated."[81] This further indicates that satisfaction marks the end of advancement. This is not always a bad thing and does not mean death is imminent. It just means someone who is satisfied is done improving, advancing, polishing, or perfecting the task at hand. Satisfaction should be judiciously mixed with the *law of diminishing returns*.[82] Some things

---

[80] Colossians 2:19

[81] The Amplified Bible. *Satiated*: satisfied to the point of boredom. *The Holy Bible: The Amplified Bible*. 1987. 2015. La Habra, CA: The Lockman Foundation.

[82] Benefits that beyond a certain point fail to increase or improve in proportion to the work extended.

are never going to improve, and at that point it is better to be satisfied than to go insane trying to achieve the impossible. On the other hand, many people have been able to beat terminal diseases and other dire odds because they were *not* satisfied and wanted to accomplish more in life.

By contrast, *contentment* implies you desire much more, but you choose to be joyful in your present condition, knowing fully well you will not remain there forever. Paul addressed contentment in Philippians 4:11-12 (NASB):

> **[11]Not that I speak from want, for I have learned to be content[83] in whatever circumstances I am. [12]I know how to get along with humble means (poverty), and I also know how to live in prosperity; in any and every circumstance I have learned the secret of being filled and going hungry, both of having abundance and suffering need.**

Paul was not one to ever be satisfied. He was a man on fire for God who burned his candle at both ends in order to see his Savior face to face. I am sure there were times his personal drive was tremendously frustrated by the limitation of the technologies of his day and the inconsistencies of the churches' support. Never one to settle for the status quo of satisfaction, Paul had to learn contentment.

Contentment is an attitude that we must learn in order to maintain joy in our God-ordained station in life. Without contentment, we would probably quit the tough times for something easier, or we would quit the lean times for something that promises more. Paul's exhortation reminds us that both poverty *and* prosperity require a learned skill to navigate. Without the wise attitude of contentment, both poverty and prosperity present the believer with dangerous extremes. As Agur requested, "give me neither poverty nor riches." The key is to learn contentment. Paul also contrasted the two extremes of provision in verse 12:

---

[83] Greek *autarkes—self-sufficient,* literally self-strengthened.

- Poverty—Contentment knows how to be filled while hungry. Joy in the face of lack is difficult and must be learned.
- Abundance—Dissatisfaction desires more even when it has abundance. Hunger in the face of abundance is difficult and must also be learned.

Paul recognized the difficulty of the balanced walk he had learned to demonstrate when he declared in Philippians 4:13, "I can do all things through Christ who strengthens me." Do what things? Be content when I have nothing, or when I have everything I could ever desire, be hungry for greater things.

Though this last point may sound like greed, Jesus addressed the dangers of Kingdom satisfaction with the parable of *The Rich Fool*.[84] The rich fool's sin was not his wealth but his desire to take his ease once he achieved a certain level of wealth. Contrary to Paul's teaching, the rich fool failed to maintain a hunger for more—not more for himself, but more for God. As Luke 12:21 concludes, "So is he that layeth up treasure for himself, and is not rich toward God." The call of the Gospel will never allow you to settle for less. There is always more territory to possess for the Kingdom.

Station Identification

No doubt about it, the hyper-prosperity message paints the picture that God wants everyone to live like kings. The prosperity message began pure enough in the 1970s with well-intentioned ministers teaching God's people that poverty wasn't a sign of holiness and that God's Word promised divine provision. Unfortunately, the message grew untamed, fertilized by the baby-boomer generation's growing appetite for stuff. The problem with the message is that while it brought forth needed understanding concerning the reward system tied to giving,[85] it neglected common sense doctrines like stewardship, budgeting, and self-control. Before long, the prosperity message looked more like a golden-

---

[84] See Luke 12:16-21.
[85] That there is a biblical reward system tied to material giving is indisputable. See Genesis 14:17-20; Proverbs 3:9-10; 11:24-25; Malachi 3:10-12; Luke 6:38; 2 Corinthians 9:6-10; and Hebrews 7:1-7.

lotto-scratch-off ticket that you had to give offerings to acquire—every ticket was a million-dollar winner, but you had to play to win. This aberration of doctrine failed to recognize that God does not call everybody to the same station in life.

Let's be honest, if we assume all Christians pursue the plan of God for their life, a husband and wife both called by God to be educators will never see the same kind of provision they would have had God called them to be lawyers. In terms of annual income, teachers live at a lower station in this life than do lawyers. But what a teaching couple would lack in terms of income when compared to a lawyer couple, they would make up for in their ability to spend time together or have more time with their children. Lawyers, arguably, work 90 hours a week year-round, and though there is a greater financial benefit, other areas of their life will be strained. There will always be a trade-off somewhere. Teachers should never try to compare their *daily bread* to that of lawyers. Nor should doctors compare their generous *daily bread* to that of successful entrepreneurs. It's just not reasonable.

To summarize, young people should diligently seek God in their career pursuits, understanding that He is *not* obligated to finance their personal agendas, only His master plan. God's provision is always tied to His plan. Find His plan in order to access His provision. Be content where God has called you, knowing He will never leave you nor forsake you. Identify your station in life and stay in your lane as you run your race.

My Ministry Station In Life

This concept may better be explained with a real, howbeit extreme, example. Several years ago, I was visiting my dear cousin in Texas. At the time, my cousin was a youth pastor on staff at one of the biggest churches in America. In that season, the church's attendance was just over 30,000 people. He offered to give my wife and I a tour of the church's grounds to which we gladly accepted. The size of this church, its grounds, and its wealth is really hard to communicate. I don't think I knew such churches existed (and mind you, this was not a seeker-friendly church growing due to compromised, feel-good, easy-believism.

This church and their pastor still preach the uncompromised Gospel and do so wearing a suit and tie.).

After an hour or so tour, we eventually made our way to the 8,000-seat sanctuary (our church seats a fraction of that). As we entered, I immediately noticed two things: 1) there was a young man, maybe early twenties, working in the sound booth to my left and 2) straight-ahead were the two biggest television cameras I had ever seen. They were the size of cameras I had seen on the game show *The Price is Right* as a child. My cousin introduced me to the young sound technician as his pastor-cousin from Tennessee. The young man noticed I was investigating the dual television cameras. He asked if I was on television, to which I replied in the affirmative (we were on two small local cable access channels).

As I climbed up onto the camera stand and gripped the handles of the camera, I observed that the camera operator's viewfinder was much larger than our whole camera. Just for grins, I asked the young tech the price of the monstrous camera with which I was toying. Without missing a beat, he stated, "Well the real expense is in the lenses since it's high-definition, so the camera is only about $250,000, but the lens is about half a million, so all together it's about $750,000." "Cool," I nodded as if I expected it to be about that. Then I asked the price of the camera stand. About $60,000. I looked around the sanctuary and counted eight cameras. I don't remember if they were all of the same price and caliber as the two I was looking at, but at that moment I got a real good sense of how broad a spectrum God's Kingdom encompasses: from the humble sandwich-boarded street preacher all the way up to a mega-church with no less than $5 million in sanctuary camera equipment.

The young sound tech then asked if I was in the market for new cameras, to which I again replied in the affirmative. (We were looking at the next generation of HD cameras from Sony. Price: just under $1,000.) It struck me that it didn't faze him that I might be looking to buy a $750,000 camera. The whole scenario was normal to him. This was everyday ministry to him. The entire conversation was surreal to me.

Here I was, a pastor of relatively humble means, sitting at the king's table. Evidently, his pleasant bread included an 8,000-seat sanctuary and some serious multimedia equipment. Everything on this king's table was orders of magnitude greater than anything I had ever seen or been around. But it was just such a situation for which Proverbs 23:1-5 had been written.

Here the wisdom of God warned me to put a knife to my throat if I was a man given to appetite, but I can honestly say none of it elicited or awakened any grandiose desires in me. I was neither jealous nor envious of these ministry dainties. I could clearly see that God had assigned the senior pastor and his ministry to a much higher station than I had been appointed. A station I did not begrudge him at all. His pleasant bread was not a temptation to me. I was honored to be at the table, howbeit briefly, and then return to the convenient bread God had given me in Tennessee.

I will never pastor 30,000 people. I will never require an 8,000-seat sanctuary. I will never require $5 million in sanctuary camera equipment. It is just not my portion in life. This does not bother me a bit. I am still busy doing everything God has tasked me with, and my plate stays very full. (No pun intended.) Kingdom success is measured by obedience, not by numbers.

As we finished up the sanctuary tour, I didn't want to mislead the young soundman into thinking I was on par with this level of ministry, so I had to clear things up. I looked at the young man and said something to the effect, "Just so you know, I'm in the process of negotiating for the purchase of my church building. My church occupies 18,000 sq. feet of historic storefront, and just one of these cameras would pay for my entire church building and the parking lot. And your camera's viewfinder is much bigger than the cameras we currently use." He shrugged, "That's cool."

Keeping Up With The Joneses (A Race For The Discontent)

I don't know who the Joneses are, but they apparently have bottomless coffers. They never seem to run out of money. They always have the latest fashion and the nicest, newest car. They have the biggest home and take the most luxurious vacations. Their kids are involved in every activity. They seem to always have tickets to some major sporting event and gear for every hobby and sport under the sun. They sure seem to be blessed, but it might be difficult for me to be friends with them. I don't think we would have much in common.

The Bible actually warns us about sitting down to dinner with people like the Joneses. Oh, the Bible doesn't call them "the Joneses" or even something Jewish sounding like the Jonesites or the Bar-Joneses, but the Bible does caution us to never compare ourselves among ourselves, for doing so is not wise.[86] In order to keep up with the Joneses, we have to measure our self-worth in accordance with their possessions. All this really does is diminish our value and keep us playing middle school, social games. If you recall, God promised to supply our daily needs, not our daily wants; so, many people may be suffering financial lack because they squandered their *daily bread* on keeping up appearances with the Joneses.

The Bible exhorts us to contentment. Contentment is being joyful where you are on the way to where you are going. A wise steward lives beneath their means. Contentment is key to obeying your budget and living beneath your means. Jesus commanded the Roman soldiers to be content with their wages.[87] Paul said he had to learn how to be content;[88] therefore, contentment is a heart attitude that we must learn. Paul exhorted Timothy to be content with food and clothing because godliness with contentment is great gain.[89] Hebrews teaches us that the opposite of contentment is covetousness.[90] God does not supply the funds necessary to keep up with the Joneses. If you live in constant debt, you may be wasting your *daily bread* on trying to sit at King Jones' table.

Pastoral Experience

Since 2010, I begin every January by teaching a financial stewardship Sunday School. This is typically an eight-week course. I do this to build the faith of our congregation so they can charge the New Year with a fresh discipline and renewed understanding of their fiscal responsibilities. Over the years, I have watched singles and families come out of debt and begin

---

[86] 2 Corinthians 10:12
[87] Luke 3:14
[88] Philippians 4:11
[89] 1 Timothy 6:6, 8
[90] Hebrews 13:5

to prosper. Others have continued to circle the mountain of financial ruin. I would be remiss if I did not include my observations of where Christians commonly hurt themselves financially, usually in trying to keep up with the Joneses.

- Cars—Just because your budget has breathing room for the car payment does not mean you will be able to afford the new car insurance, the higher car maintenance, or the difference in gas mileage. Don't be car-broke.
- Technology—You don't need the latest smartphone or a bigger TV. Cellphone data plans can break a lot of budgets. And who said your 10-year-old needs a smartphone with unlimited data? Cable plans and other monthly entertainment subscriptions, like streaming services, quickly add up.
- Food—I have observed many believers break their budget on dining out[91] and overeating. Dining out is convenient but costly. Overeating wastes money on unnecessary calories.
- Pets—If you cannot afford to tithe, you can't afford a pet. Will a man rob God to feed his dog? Absolutely! This is idolatry. The average American spends $127 every month on a single pet.[92] Over one-third of American households have pets.[93]
- Vacations—Vacations are typically stressful, busy, expensive, and require recuperation time upon return. Contrary to Western beliefs, you don't need a vacation and you certainly don't need to go into debt to take one. If you can afford one, great! But do not go into debt trying to follow the Joneses to Disney. You will only return exhausted and stressed over all of the newly acquired debt.

---

[91] The first year my wife and I pastored, we both worked full-time jobs outside of the church. We didn't know much about pastoring or flock care, but we ate out after every service with different church members. Our food expenditures for that first year were $9,000. Needless to say, we changed that very quickly.

[92] https://www.businessinsider.com/how-much-it-costs-to-own-dog-cat-other-pets-2018-4

[93] Ibid.

- Houses—Many Christians have harmed themselves by mortgaging a home they cannot afford. Like automobiles, there is much more to a home's cost than just the monthly mortgage. Don't forget about utilities, lawn care, upkeep, insurance, and property taxes. God wants you to have a home; He just doesn't want you to be house-broke.
- Bonuses and Raises—Finally, too often Christians increase their means of living every time they get a raise or a bonus. Wisdom requires that extra money be used to pay down debt or increase savings.

Conclusion

Get a budget. Stick with it. Be thankful for your *daily bread* and your *convenient bread*. Should God see fit to promote you to higher stations in life, be thankful, but use it to advance the Kingdom. Should you only be a mere guest at the king's table, watch your heart and your appetites. Many people want the bread that belongs to a higher station, but they have never contentedly mastered their current position. There are increases and promotions to be had in Christ, but they won't come without contentment and stewardship. Be content with such things as you have. Wisdom also says have a savings account. Don't feel obligated to empty your savings every offering. Have an inheritance for your children's children. This will require a long-term financial vision. Don't live paycheck to paycheck and certainly don't live for the weekend. Lift up your eyes—look further into the future than this Saturday. And don't go into debt for a vacation.

- Do you have a budget? When will you start?
- Do you obey your budget? When will you start?
- Have you identified your station in life? Have you learned to be faithful there?
- Are you content as you pursue greater things or have you cooled off into satisfaction?
- Are you pursuing the Joneses or Jesus Christ?

Minister's Moment

As a minister of the Gospel, you must be a living example of righteous doctrine. This means that your personal money and your ministerial money must be disciplined. As a minister, you work for God and you live by the altar, but the same rules of budgeting and self-control apply to you as well. Do not expect your people to flourish financially if you don't. How you live privately preaches louder than your public sermons. Do you have a budget for personal finances? Do you live beneath your means? Does your ministry have a budget? How will you know what to ask God for if you don't have a budget? Are you steering your ministry to keep up with the Rev. Jones (what if he turns out to be Jim Jones)? Never forget, God trusts you with the widow's mite and real prosperity begins with a budget.

CHAPTER 7

APPETITE DISCIPLINE
(HOW TO BEAT "FAT")

Isn't life more than food . . . ?   *-Matthew 6:25 (NLT)*

Put a knife to your throat if you are given to gluttony.
-Proverbs 23:2 (NIV)

Several years ago I was at the beach with some friends. We were in Florida for a church conference and the afternoon afforded us a few hours to visit the ocean. As we were leaving the beach that day to head back to the hotel and get cleaned up for the evening meetings, a rather obese twenty-something lady walked in front of our vehicle preventing us from making a turn we needed to make. She was wearing one of those large Hawaiian muumuu swimsuit covers, perhaps not so much for modesty as out of insecurity about her size. As I observed her, it seemed to me that though she was at the beach and had been in a swimsuit, she was still very self-conscious about her weight. She was also moving slowly, and I could see that her gait was strained due to her size.

As I took all of this in, and as we waited for her to slowly pass in front of our car so we could continue on our way, I impatiently said in my heart, "Maybe if you weren't so big, you could walk a little faster." No sooner had my heart whispered that ridicule when the Word of the Lord came to me and gently asked, "What would you say to her if that was Lydia in 20 years (my oldest daughter who was 5 years old at the time)?" My mind suddenly created a picture of my beloved first daughter, 20 years older, no longer healthy, active, and confident, but overweight, insecure, and swallowed up by the specter of discouragement. My heart sank and I instantly repented. I was filled with shame for myself, but also compassion and sympathy for this young lady.

I answered the Lord, "Father, I would encourage her, and love her, and help her in any way I could to lose weight, get healthy, and regain her confidence."

I share this story to hopefully communicate that this chapter is not about what is beautiful and what is ugly. This is not a chapter meant to "fat-shame" anyone. In fact, the metric of beauty is defined differently all over the world. For example, take sumo wrestlers. Though they are considered obese by Western standards, sumos are actually well-respected and adored elite athletes in Japan. Likewise, many African cultures prize full-figured women. In their eyes, obesity is a sign of wealth.

We were once cared for in West Africa by a very regal and stately sister-in-Christ from the church hosting us. She was a very successful banker married to a very successful businessman. They were both leaders in our host church and were tremendous servants at heart. This dear saint was tall, lean, composed, and very beautiful. She is what my Western mind would imagine an African queen to look like. One day, my wife and I inquired of the pastor and his wife concerning this lady and her family. After he shared a brief synopsis of their life and testimony, he made the comment, "It's just a pity she is so skinny. She can't seem to put on any weight." This was said as if to imply that all of her strengths and successes were negated by the fact that she was too skinny for their cultural taste. Though my wife and I agreed this lady was very beautiful by Western standards, her culture viewed her as the ugly duckling.

Even our missionary friends in Uganda have experienced this discrepancy in cultural taste. Upon returning from a two-month stateside furlough, their Ugandan friends rejoiced to see how "fat" they had gotten. One dear Ugandan sister even greeted the missionary wife with, "Oh my goodness. You got so fat. And it looks so good on you." At which point the Americans began their detox.

A Matter Of Health

First and foremost, this is a chapter about health and long life. This is also a chapter about self-discipline and the confidence self-discipline can bring. Obesity is a sensitive subject for many Westerners, tied to so much insecurity, shame, and depression. My own primary care physician related to me that he has great difficulty speaking to some of his patients about their weight due to their insecurity and sensitivity. Clearly, he is coming to them not to shame them or ridicule them, but with the care and concern of a medical professional to aid and relieve them. Yet, he related to me how some of his patients shut him down and were offended that he would dare try to address their weight. We both agreed that offended people cannot be helped.

Our modern culture has evolved new benchmarks for beauty and desirability. These are norms that reject larger, fuller bodies. Many of these standards did not exist even 100 years ago. Any casual student of art appreciation will quickly notice that the Renaissance artists of old painted and sculpted a much more full-figured woman than is generally found to be attractive today. Other cultures pursue and elevate both men and women of larger builds. These facts might remind us of the old adage, "Beauty is in the eye of the beholder." And though there are some men (and women) in the West that favor a mate with, as one man said, "a little bit of meat on her bones," the overall society disagrees. But this is not a chapter about what is beautiful. This is a chapter about what is healthy.

Obesity Is Not God's Will

Obesity is not God's will. Not only can obesity make many aspects of normal day-to-day life more difficult than necessary, it can also devastate a person's self-confidence and morale. Some have become so hopeless in their endeavor to lose weight they have discarded wisdom, science, and health in order to embrace their obesity in social movements such as "fat activism" and body positivity mantras like "fat is beautiful." Despite these current cultural pushes to make fat beautiful and acceptable, most rational people understand that the concern with obesity is not a matter of beauty or acceptance, but one of immediate day-to-day health and long-term quality of life.

The medical causes behind the obesity epidemic are varied and complex. Much research is still being performed on them, and are therefore well beyond the scope of this book. A brief list of the causes of obesity would include medical conditions, genetic conditions, diet, lifestyle, and emotional traumas like childhood sexual, physical, and emotional abuse. The medical community looks at these causes and endeavors to treat obesity through drugs, surgery, lifestyle training, and counseling. I am not a medical expert, so I do not portend to offer medical advice or recommend any kind of surgery or drug prescription. I would encourage readers to listen to and heed their doctor's/therapist's counsel.

What I am is a Bible teacher and author, so I will address obesity from a biblical and doctrinal perspective, and therefore offer wisdom and doctrine from the Holy Scriptures. It is my hope and prayer that something in this chapter, if mixed with professional wisdom and medicine, might work to set at liberty those who are bound. But first, a bit of medical science might be in order.

Medical Background

Physicians use a body mass index or BMI[1] to quantify a person's body mass and then medically classify them on a scale ranging from *Underweight* to *Obese*. While there is a total of eleven categories on the BMI scale, it must be noted that the *Obese* end of the scale has six sub-categories ranging from *Obese* to *Hyper Obese*.

Currently, both the IRS and Medicare maintain language recognizing obesity as a disease.[2] While obesity has always been classified as a "condition" or a "disorder," in 2013 the American Medical Association (AMA) voted to officially recognize obesity as a disease. This decision was not without controversy due to this logical implication: if obesity is a disease, then it is a self-inflicted disease that can be reversed. Furthermore, if obesity is a disease, what does that do to the social movements fighting to declare "fat is beautiful"? Have we really come to a place in Western culture where, for the sake of eking out some level of self-confidence, we want to declare that a potential life-threatening disease is "beautiful"?[3]

---

[1] BMI is controversial among physicians due to its oversimplification of individual health. The newest index proposed is called the Body Volume Indicator (BVI).

[2] https://www.medicalnewstoday.com/articles/262226.php

[3] I understand the psychology behind such a statement. Having given up the fight to get healthy, what can one do to avoid being swallowed up by shame and misery but embrace what is truly harmful.

According to a 2017 Fortune Magazine article, based upon BMI, 70% of Americans classify as either overweight or obese and nearly 40% of Americans are obese.[4] Obesity is directly linked to cancer, heart disease, diabetes, hypertension, stroke, sleep apnea, lymphedema, and dementia. Even sadder is the fact that the childhood obesity rate in America stands at 20% and continues to rise.[5] Obese children are more likely to develop chronic health conditions, including type 2 diabetes, sleep apnea, bone and joint problems, and asthma, to say nothing of the mental anguish, isolation, depression, and lower self-esteem they will likely develop from the bullying they are all but guaranteed to endure. And in fulfillment of a Bible proverb, obese parents are more likely to have obese children.[6] In fact, a child with one obese parent has a 50% chance of being obese. But if both parents are obese, the child's risk of obesity increases to 80%.[7]

We Simply Weren't Made For This

It is painfully evident from the many diseases tied to obesity that the human body is simply not designed to be overweight. Yes, the body is designed to store some fat for later use, but not such large reservoirs as to kill us. Obesity taxes almost every aspect of our body, from the cardiovascular and the pulmonary systems to the digestive system and skin. Perhaps most critical is the burden obesity places on an individual's heart.

When exhorting my church about their personal health and self-control, I often have our church members make a fist, place it to their chest, and then look down to understand how large their heart is in comparison to the rest of their body. Your fist is approximately the size of your heart. Without too large a margin of difference, every person's fist is roughly the same size, yet our bodies are not within the same margin of difference.

The human heart is often likened to a car engine. Generally speaking, our hearts are a modest four-cylinder engine trying to power

---

[4] http://fortune.com/2017/10/13/obesity-in-america/
[5] Ibid.
[6] Ezekiel 16:44
[7] https://www.ucsfbenioffchildrens.org/conditions/obesity/ (accessed 7/2019)

anything in size ranging from a huge Mack truck to a healthier-sized compact car. I think the analogy makes itself clear. A four-cylinder engine is designed for use in powering a compact car, but grossly insufficient for a Mack truck and will eventually result in a blown engine (heart attack).

If we continue with the analogy of vehicles, each of us has a "chassis" or frame called a skeleton, and again, they are all very close in size and proportion. The frame of a modest compact car was designed to safely—and with a significant factor of safety—carry the load for which it was designed. It was never intended to carry the load of a Mack truck or even a large van. Human bones can adjust to a degree but will eventually begin to distort under unnecessary weight. More critical is that joints will prematurely break down, often calling for steroid shots to temporarily relieve pain or, worst-case scenario, require joint replacement surgery.

Obesity even over-taxes the skin, stretching it beyond its limit, resulting in scarring and loose skin. Other clinical entities are common to the majority of obese patients, e.g. stretch marks, plantar hyperkeratosis (corns and calluses on the feet), and an increased risk of skin infections. It may also be associated with poor wound healing, malignant melanoma, and an increased risk of inflammatory dermatoses, such as psoriasis, as well as other rare disorders.

I think we can see God never intended for our bodies to grow as large as modern society has recently pushed the envelope. Modern culture, with its sedentary lifestyle, unhealthy diet, depression and insecurity, and childhood traumas, has pushed the human body to its breaking point one meal at a time. We have unintentionally experimented on our own bodies to see what is possible. Can the human body still function at levels of obesity? Sure. Thirty percent of America proves that every day, but this represents a body at its extreme-most limits, near its breaking point, and not a body operating at its optimum levels or peak performance.

But, of course, you probably already know most of this. The problem is that for some reason, the Church doesn't really touch on this aspect of the Christian walk. Maybe it's because the Church is also

30%[8] obese, and we don't want to hurt anybody's feelings. We would rather just bury them prematurely and comfort their loved ones after the fact. Or maybe it's because the typical preacher is also overweight himself, if not obese, and it's one sin he cannot hide. No preacher in his or her right mind is going to publically preach against a sin they are so clearly and unrepentantly guilty of.

How can the Church get victory over obesity if they are never taught about self-control? How can a preacher declare he has preached the whole counsel of God's Word if he shies away from the cultural sin of gluttony? We claim we believe faith can move mountains, but what if that mountain is our own body? Faith comes by hearing and hearing the Word of God. Faith to move the mountain of obesity must be developed by preaching the doctrine of self-control and the message that obesity is not the will of God.

As a simple review, here is a list of many of the diseases and medical complications associated with or directly caused by obesity:

- Cancer
- Type II diabetes
- Joint breakdown
- Stroke
- Lymphedema
- Poor wound healing
- Inflammatory dermatoses
- Heart disease
- Hypertension
- Stretch marks
- Sleep apnea
- Dementia
- Malignant melanoma

The Western Food Obsession

To revisit the subject of culture, only in America do we have a television network called the Food Network dedicated to 24-hour food-related programing, and just two clicks away you can find a TV show called *My 600-lb Life*. And on the same channel *My Big Fat Fabulous Life*. We treat hunger pangs like dental checkups—to be avoided at all costs. Someone pointed out that we are a society that travels with snacks in our glove compartments, purses, and backpacks, just in case we can't make it

---

[8] If not more than 30%—seriously. Christians fellowship around food and potluck dinners.

to the next meal. Remember, America invented the 44 oz.[9] Super Big Gulp fountain drink—7-Eleven's greatest contribution to pop-culture—the 64 oz. Double Big Gulp, and now the 150 oz. X-Gulp (that's 1 gallon, ladies and gentlemen)! America even inadvertently invented the all-you-can-eat buffet in order to keep Vegas gamblers going.[10] Not to be outdone by the ingenuity of the Vegas casino buffets, county fairs all across America have entered into a bizarre arms race of one-upmanship in the sport of deep-fried foods, including deep-fried Oreos, deep-fried candy bars, and now deep-fried sticks of butter. Seriously?! This is to say nothing of Major League Eating (MLE) and the Professional League of Eating Contests. (It's a real thing. Look it up!)

We now have a segment of Western society that self-identifies as "foodies," that is, a person who has a passionate interest in the latest food fads and new restaurants. Food fads? Yes, food fads. And just what is that you may be asking? Don't ask me for examples because I'm not a foodie, but I imagine $8 designer cupcakes, $4 gourmet donuts, Frappuccinos, and a deep-fried stick of butter probably qualify.

It was just 30 years ago we were trying to feed the people of Africa,[11] but that fad grew old and the Ethiopian famine of 1983-85 passed, so now we just find delicious ways to entertain ourselves. This is due in part to the West's abundant prosperity. The days of subsistence farming passed with the advent of the Industrial Revolution. We no longer have to plow sunup to sundown just to go to bed with a full belly. As we saw in Chapter 6, the West's Christian foundation has afforded it unprecedented prosperity and like Jeshurun, we have "waxed fat,"[12] both figuratively and literally. Our technologies have given us plenty of free time we as a society have used to invent the hobby of eating and food photography. I have never seen someone in Botswana or the bush of Kenya take a picture of their dinner just to post it on social media—#mopaneworm, #matoke. But then again, those countries don't have an obesity epidemic.

---

[9] The average human stomach can only hold 32 oz. at any given time.
[10] A man named Herb McDonald working at the El Rancho casino in Las Vegas developed the first all-you-can-eat buffet. Mr. McDonald commercialized the Swedish smörgåsbord, and for $1 (this was the 1940s) you could eat your fill at the "Buckaroo Buffet."
[11] Live Aid, Band Aid, and United Song Artists (USA) for Africa.
[12] Deuteronomy 32:15

Obesity In The Bible

There are only four obese people named in the Bible: the Moabite King Eglon, the Israelite High Priest Eli, and his two sons, Hophni and Phineas. The first two met bizarre deaths related to their obesity. Hophni and Phineas died in battle.

When the Israelite Judge Ehud assassinated King Eglon with an 18-inch dagger, the Bible specifically notes that the dagger could not be retracted because Eglon was "a very fat man" and his fat had swallowed the entire dagger.[13] The way the Bible narrative reads here, it sounds as though King Eglon might have survived the assassination had he been able to retrieve the dagger, but then again, maybe not. Also, consider that he was so large, an 18-inch dagger was lost in his fat. This definitely describes what is considered today as morbidly obese.

Concerning the High Priest Eli, God rebuked him for being dishonorable toward Him. Eli and his two sons had dishonored God by becoming obese on the peoples' offerings. The rebuke had several aspects to it:

> **Why do you [all] scorn my sacrifice and offering that I prescribed for my dwelling? Why do you honor your sons more than me by fattening yourselves on the choice parts of every offering made by my people Israel?**
> **1 Samuel 2:29 (NIV)**

When God asks a human being a question, it is never for His benefit. God always asks questions to reveal the sinful condition of the heart in order to bring about repentance. Here God asks Eli two questions:

1. Why do you and your sons disrespect My prescribed sacrifice and offerings?
2. Why do you honor your sons more than Me by making yourselves fat with the best part of all the [meat] offerings?

---

[13] See Judges 3:21-22.

How were they disrespecting God's offerings and dishonoring Him? By literally fattening themselves with the choicest parts of meat offerings. The priests were allowed by God to eat of the offerings the people brought.[14] This was one of the ways in which the Levites were cared for. But Eli and his sons had fallen into the dishonorable habit of taking more offering than was necessary for their sustenance to the point of obesity. God called all three of them fat! Their obesity was a sign of their greed. They lacked self-control and they kept stealing from God's offerings to feed their insatiable appetites.

Though Hophni and Phineas were also sexual perverts, seducing the female servants to sleep with them,[15] the anger of God was stirred up over their disrespect for His offerings. The judgment of God was set against this family of priests, declared by an unnamed man of God, and confirmed later by Samuel. Oddly enough, many years passed between the declaration of the judgment and its fulfillment, perhaps as many as 10 years. The Philistines killed both Hophni and Phineas in the same day. When their father Eli received the report that his sons had been killed in battle and the Ark of the Covenant had been stolen, he fell over backwards and "broke his neck and died, for he was old and over-weight."[16]

Old Testament Exhortations

For the purpose of building our faith, let us consider several passages from the Old Testament. How does the Law view overeating? Consider this passage from Deuteronomy (emphasis added):

> **[18]If any man has a stubborn and rebellious son who will not obey his father or his mother, and when they chastise him, he will not even listen to them, [19]then his father and mother shall seize him, and bring him out to the elders of his city at the gateway of his hometown. [20]They shall say to the elders of his city, 'This son of ours is stubborn and rebellious, he will not obey us, he is a glutton and a drunkard.' [21]Then all the men of his city shall stone him**

---

[14] See 1 Samuel 2:12-17 (NASB).
[15] 1 Samuel 2:22
[16] 1 Samuel 4:18 (NLT)

to death; <u>so you shall remove the evil from your midst</u>,
and all Israel will hear of it and fear.
Deuteronomy 21:18-21 (NASB)

The heart of this passage is not to stone disobedient children, as progressive theologians are apt to proclaim (what a horrible misapplication of the passage). The passage reveals that the purpose behind the commandment is "so shall you remove the evil from your midst" as an example to everyone else. But what is the evil? Stubbornness, rebellion, and disobedience. And how are stubbornness, rebellion, and disobedience demonstrated in this passage? They are demonstrated by gluttony and drunkenness. Gluttony and drunkenness are linked together by the Law of God. And just as a reminder, gluttony is excessive eating. The Law of Moses equates excessive eating to drunkenness and deems both of them as evil. One makes you drunk. The other makes you fat. Both represent a lack of self-control. The solution, according to God, is to "remove the evil from your midst."

Proverbs continues in harmony with Moses, linking gluttony and drunkenness together. Solomon's wisdom offers a prohibition and a warning:

> [20]**Do not be with heavy drinkers of wine, Or with gluttonous eaters of meat;** [21]**For the heavy drinker and the glutton will come to poverty, And drowsiness will clothe one with rags.** **Proverbs 23:20-21 (NASB)**

> **He who keeps the law is a discerning son, But he who is a companion of gluttons humiliates his father.**
> **Proverbs 28:7 (NASB)**

These proverbs forbid even friendship with gluttons. Wow! That may seem harsh, but God is looking out for the best interest of His people. He also gives reasons why we should not fellowship with drunks and gluttons—they will come to poverty. Bad company corrupts good morals.[17] There is also a spiritual law echoed here, as throughout the Bible—you will become what you behold.[18] We must be cautious who we fellowship with. These two proverbs alone will also prevent a Christian college student from joining a fraternity or a sorority.

Returning to Proverbs 23:1-3, if we read this passage, not considering *who* is present, e.g. the ruler, but focus now on *what* is present, the food, we can glean another bit of wisdom from it.

> **[1]When you sit down to dine with a ruler, Consider carefully what is before you, [2]And put a knife to your throat if you are a man of great appetite. [3]Do not desire his delicacies, for it is deceptive food.**
> **Proverbs 23:1-3 (NASB)**

Revisiting these verses, we can develop a very simple process for appetite control. It is hard to believe that at least 2,200 years before our modern weight loss and diet fads, Solomon had this bit of wisdom to offer when you sit down to eat:

1. Consider carefully what is before you . . .
2. If you are a big eater, put a knife to your throat . . .
3. Because food is deceptive.

Amazingly simple!! What a strategy.

New Testament Exhortations

After all we have studied so far, it should come as no surprise that the New Testament also has many things to say about food appetites and self-control.

> **[17]Now I urge you, brethren, keep your eye on those who cause dissensions and hindrances contrary to the**

---

[17] 1 Corinthians 15:33 (NASB)
[18] Jacob's cattle beheld streaked, speckled and spotted rods, and they produced streaked, speckled and spotted offspring (see Genesis 30:22-43). In the New Testament, if we will behold the glory of God, it is promised that we will be changed into the same image (2 Corinthians 3:18).

teaching which you learned, and turn away from them. ¹⁸For such men are slaves, not of our Lord Christ but of their own appetites; Romans 16:17-18a (NASB)

This is a very strong statement. Paul revealed that there will always be troublemakers in the church. One of their characteristics is that they are slaves to their own appetites. They are not slaves to Jesus. Are you a slave to your food appetites? When was the last time you skipped a meal just to do it, just to deny your flesh and deprive it pleasure?

I once served a pastor who was very tall and thin. Genetically speaking, I think he was an anomaly. He could eat anything and everything and not gain an ounce of body fat. I was privileged to dine with him on many occasions, and I can testify that he would always leave a small pile of food on his plate, perhaps just enough for a bite or two. I once asked him why he did this. His reply, "I purposely leave the last bite or two just to tell my flesh, 'No! You don't win. I win.'" This was foreign to me because, as a proper Southerner, I was brought up to always clean my plate. And as I have previously stated, my pastor was a very lean man and did not struggle with his weight. So to understand his purpose in always leaving a bite or two is really to understand a secret to self-discipline, that is, it involves constant little acts of restraint. Constant little acts of self-control can prevent us from requiring massive life-changing interventions.

That pastor was a very disciplined man. Even in the area of food, where he did not have to be disciplined, he still chose to be disciplined. What about you? Are you capable of leaving the last bite or two behind, on the first serving of food? It doesn't count if it's seconds or thirds. By then your stomach is groaning anyway. Can you do it? Or are you more of a "no french-fry left behind" kind of eater? Is your appetite your master?

The previous passage in Romans addresses troublemakers in the church. The following passage from Philippians exposes a different kind of character—the enemy of the cross. These people are not the same as church troublemakers because their judgment is not the same. Church troublemakers are to be avoided and shunned. The enemies of the cross will be destroyed. That is a very big difference.

> [18] For I have often told you, and now say again with tears, that many live as enemies of the cross of Christ. [19] Their end is destruction; <u>their god is their stomach</u>; their glory is in their shame. <u>They are focused on earthly things</u>, [20] but our citizenship is in heaven, and we eagerly wait for a Savior from there, the Lord Jesus Christ.
>
> **Philippians 3:18-20 (CSB) (emphases added)**

The other difference between church troublemakers and enemies of the cross is their relationship with their stomach. Troublemakers are slaves to their stomach. Enemies of the cross worship their stomach. Their stomach is their god and they are focused on earthly things. Let us be honest, it takes a lot of work to get obese and then stay there. It's a labor. It takes a lot of focus to eat enough food to maintain that size. The problem arises that the level of eating necessary to maintain an obese build becomes habit-forming. This does not imply that obese Christians are enemies of the cross, not by any means. But it cannot be overlooked that if your stomach is your god, you do have at least one thing in common with an enemy of the cross. We are to glorify God with our body, not make our body into a god.

> [19] What? know ye not that your body is the temple of the Holy Ghost which is in you, which ye have of God, and ye are not your own? [20] For ye are bought with a price: therefore glorify God in your body, and in your spirit, which are God's.
>
> **1 Corinthians 6:19-20**

The salvific work of Christ redeemed our total being—spirit, soul, and body. Though we await our new and glorified bodies to be revealed at the Resurrection, for the time being these mere jars of clay *are* the Temple of God. If we consider the Old Testament reference used here, that we are living, mobile versions of Solomon's Temple, then we can begin to understand what it entails to glorify God in our bodies. Solomon's Temple (and even Zerubbabel's to a lesser degree) was beautifully maintained. It was to be held in honor. It was to be sanctified and used for sacred things, not profane things. It was to never fall into disrepair. It was to be prized as the dwelling place of God!

These same ideas apply to our individual bodies because Jesus Christ has redeemed them each for His glory. If we are to esteem our bodies as the Israelites did God's Temple, then we are to maintain our bodies. We must hold our bodies in honor as valuable (you care for things when they are valuable). We are to sanctify our bodies and use them for sacred things, not profane things.[19] We cannot allow our bodies to fall into disrepair. We can glorify God by taking care of our bodies.

> **For physical training[20] is of some value (useful for a little), but godliness (spiritual training) is useful and of value in everything and in every way, for it holds promise for the present life and also for the life which is to come.   1 Timothy 4:8 (Amplified)[21]**

Though Paul places the emphasis of this verse on godliness and its benefit both now and in the life to come, he does not ignore the fact that physical training, or exercise, does have "some value" and is "useful for a little." Its benefits are, of course, limited to this lifetime and do not carry over into the life that is to come. I have actually heard Christians use this verse as justification for not taking care of their bodies, saying things like, "Well, what's the point of staying in shape? The Bible says exercise only 'profiteth little.'" To answer their question: the main benefit is that training your body through physical fitness will help keep you in this life a lot longer. I, for one, don't want to drop dead halfway through my spiritual race. I want to finish my course. I believe you do too!

> **[12]All things are lawful for me, but not all things are profitable. All things are lawful for me, but I will not be mastered by anything. [13]Food is for the stomach and the**

---

[19] cf. 1 Corinthians 3:17
[20] "The training of the body" -CSB.
[21] *The Holy Bible: The Amplified Bible.* 1987. 2015. La Habra, CA: The Lockman Foundation.

> stomach is for food, but God will do away with both of them.   **1 Corinthians 6:12-13 (NASB)**

Just because we find something lawful does not mean it will prove to be profitable. We must understand that food is not the problem. Not even the deep-fried stick-o-butter is the problem. It is the self-imposed slavery to food that is the problem. The Amplified Bible adds to verse 12, "I will not become the slave of anything or be brought under its power." As if to answer the hypothetical question, "Can you give us an example?" Paul continued into verse 13 by saying, "Food is for the stomach . . ." He directly identified food as a lawful item that could easily enslave.

> **But I discipline my body and make it my slave, so that, after I have preached to others, I myself will not be disqualified.**   **1 Corinthians 9:27 (NASB)**

According to Paul, an undisciplined body has the potential to be a spiritual disqualifier, even for apostles. Paul strove for bodily discipline. He began the passage by using athletic imagery like running a race, competing in the games, and boxing, all of which require severe discipline. But as he approaches the crescendo of his line of teaching, the end of an undisciplined life being that of disqualification, and the thought of being cast away being unbearable, it is as though Paul had to find an even greater level of strictness to ensure victory. And so he leaves behind athletics and jumps straight to slavery. Paul didn't just discipline his body—he enslaved it! He enslaved his appetites. Slaves lived on tightly regulated diets. They did not have access to their master's food stores at 2 a.m. They ate when and what they were permitted. Have you ever seen a picture of an obese slave? I know I haven't.

> [12]One of themselves (Cretans), a prophet of their own, said, "Cretans are always liars, evil beasts, lazy gluttons." [13]This testimony is true. For this reason reprove them severely so that they may be sound in the faith,   **Titus 1:12-13 (NASB)**

Remember this passage from back in Chapter 2? Crete had some serious cultural shortcomings. Cretans were known for being liars, evil brutes, and lazy overeaters. Evidently that culture was brought into their church, especially if Pastor Titus had been authorized to rebuke these three lifestyles. I'm sure those were some unpleasant church services and they probably lasted several months. However, it is their third testimony—lazy gluttony—that reminds me a lot of America. We understand that lying demands a strong rebuke. We would also agree that a strong rebuke is justified if a church is full of evil brutes. But if the Cretan church required a severe rebuke for being filled with lazy gluttons, isn't the American church worthy of the same message? And when would be the best time to deliver that sermon series? Before or after the Wednesday night potluck? Before the church picnic or after the pie sale?

Early Church Exhortations

Lest anyone should think that obesity, overeating, and gluttony is only a struggle for modern believers, consider some of the teachings of Clement of Alexandria.[22] Clement was an early Christian theologian and is considered to be one of the early Church Fathers. The following quotes are from his work *Christ the Instructor, Book 2 Chapter 2:*

> *"Excess, which in all things is an evil, is very highly reprehensible in the matter of food."*
>
> *"But we who seek the heavenly bread must rule the belly, which is beneath heaven, and much more the things which are agreeable to it, which God shall destroy, says the apostle, justly execrating* [to abhor, to curse] *gluttonous desires."*
>
> *"Some men, in truth, live that they may eat, as the irrational creatures, whose life is their belly, and nothing else. But the Instructor* [Christ] *enjoins us to eat that we may live."*[23]

---

[22] Also called Titus Flavius Clemens (c. 150-215 AD), he was a pupil of Tertullian, the Father of Latin Theology. Clement is considered the first Christian scholar.

[23] Man shall not live by bread alone. See Matthew 4:4 and Luke 4:4.

It appears the Christians of the 2nd Century also had to be taught to restrain their food appetites. It should encourage us that "there hath no temptation taken us but such as is common to man."[24] Jesus is still asking the hypothetical question: Isn't life more than food?[25]

The *gods* Of All Comfort

As we wrap up this chapter, I trust you will allow me to really challenge your mindset concerning food. Our God is the God of all comfort.[26] He cares for us and is mindful of what we are going through. The Lord Jesus promised He would not leave us comfortless. According to 2 Corinthians 1:4, He "comforts us in all our affliction so that we will be able to comfort those who are in any affliction with the comfort with which we ourselves are comforted by God." The Greek word for "comfort" in this passage is *parakleo—that which brings solace, consolation, refreshing, and encouragement.* We know that the Holy Spirit is the Comforter Jesus Christ promised. He is the *Paraklete* (the Comforter).

Can you imagine how the Holy Spirit must feel, having been sent on assignment by God Almighty to do what only He can do, comfort His people, only to be rejected in exchange for . . . comfort food?[27] Can you believe that some people, when given a choice between the presence of God or a Twinkie, will actually choose the Twinkie? Sure you can. We have all done it. We have all substituted brass for gold.

"Taste and see that the Lord is good."[28] "No thank you. I'll have that leftover half of the pie." We have all turned to food for a biological release rather than prayer for a spiritual remedy. We do this because we have trained ourselves to do so. We have not trained ourselves to go to God in time of need and receive His supernatural comfort—a comfort that contains peace that passes all understanding.

When Christians forget God in time of need and turn to their comfort food, do you think they remember to pray over that food? How would that prayer even sound if it was honest?

---

[24] 1 Corinthians 10:13
[25] Matthew 6:25 (NLT)
[26] 2 Corinthians 1:3
[27] Comfort food is the food people turn to in time of high anxiety.
[28] Psalm 34:8

> *"Father, in Jesus' name, I thank You for this quart of Rocky Road ice cream. Thank You for the momentary comfort this is going to bring my body as the sugar activates the dopamine reward system in my brain. I rebuke the sugar crash that is bound to happen in one hour and the guilt that will inevitably follow tomorrow. And please give me more overtime hours so I can buy some new pants, because You know the ones I have are getting kinda tight. And bless it to the nourishment of my body, and my body to Thy service. In Jesus' name, Amen!"*

Gosh! For all that praying we might as well have just prayed about the situation that had us stressed out and emotionally taxed. But you know what? I don't think we ever bother to pray over our comfort food. I think deep down inside we know we have temporarily turned our back on God in order to seek comfort from another source.

God is a jealous God. He does not share His glory nor does He permit idolatry. How it must grieve Him as He extends a hand to His struggling children, only to watch them turn aside to food. I cannot imagine any of my children needing help and not immediately looking to their mother or me in that dire moment, especially if we were right there. If my son were to fall and bloody his knee, look up at me with tears in his little eyes, and then run right past me to an ice cream cone—I'm not sure how I would feel. Anything we turn to in time of need is our god. Who is the god of your comfort? A hotdog never delivered anyone. We must train our hearts to look to God, from whom our salvation—our total deliverance—comes.

Obesity vs. Homosexuality

I recently read an article on a secular website[29] calling upon conservative Christians to extend some compassion toward homosexuals. Oddly enough, the author chose to compare homosexuality to obesity. Several indicting observations were made: 1) "If gluttony is a sin, and prayer is the answer, it seems strange that the most religious part of the country [the

---

[29] http://www.thewrap.com/duck-dynasty-defenders-committed-sin-gluttony-opinion/ (accessed August 2019)

Bible Belt] is also the most obese;" 2) Christians expect homosexuals to pray the gay away but can't seem to pray their fat away; and 3) Religious leaders hardly ever speak out against obesity like they do homosexuality, but the Bible condemns gluttony three-to-one over homosexuality. I hate it when the heathen can see our doctrinal foibles.[30] I might just jump in while there's blood in the water and ask two questions: Don't we believe homosexuality is a choice? Is not obesity also a choice?

Oddly enough, the article did not deny that the Bible condemns homosexuality as a sin. The author did not even condemn Christians for being anti-gay. He was just voicing his frustration with the Church's hypocrisy. I must admit, it was an argument that set me back on my heels for a brief moment, and I even wondered if his stats were right. Are there three times as many scriptures against obesity/gluttony as there are against homosexuality? You know what? They were wrong. It's not three-to-one obesity over homosexuality. Based on my study, it's closer to two-to-one, homosexuality over obesity.[31] (You can't blame pagans for getting it wrong. Their knowledge of the Bible is limited to the echo chamber of a Google search.) But lest we take our ease and disregard these stats because homosexuality is condemned more often, we cannot forget God's Word condemns them both. I'm certainly not trying to conflate the two sins as identical—they are not the same. Nor does the Bible reserve the same kind of judgment for both of them—it does not, for they are *not* equal sins. But the fact remains, they are both appetite-driven sins. They both work to destroy the body; one is a sexual perversion, the other a slow suicide. But the two do share a common link: childhood sexual trauma.[32] Both

---

[30] It has been observed that God didn't destroy Sodom and Gomorrah for obesity, but Ezekiel 16:49 reveals that the sins of Sodom included "pride, abundance of bread, and abundance of idleness." The last two are a recipe for obesity (no pun intended).

[31] Scriptures condemning homosexuality: Gen. 18:20-21; 19; Lev. 18:22-24; 20:13; Deut. 23:17-18 (v.18's "dog" is Hebrew for homosexual prostitute); Judges 19:22; 1 Kings 14:24; 15:12; 22:46; 2 Kings 23:7. New Testament: Rom. 1:26-32; 1 Cor. 6:9, 18; Jude 1:7. If we interpret *pornos* to include (in context) homosexuality, then we can include 1 Cor. 5:9-11; Eph. 5:5; Heb. 12:16; 13:4; and Rev. 21:8.

Scriptures condemning obesity: Deut. 21:18-21; 1 Sam. 2:29; Prov. 23:1-3, 20-21; 28:7. New Testament (appetite cautions): Rom. 16:17-18; 1 Cor. 3:17; 6:12-13; 9:27; 1 Tim. 4:8; Titus 1:12-13.

[32] Research in 2001 found that 46% of gay men reported childhood homosexual molestation, https://www.ncbi.nlm.nih.gov/m/pubmed/11501300/#.

homosexuality and obesity have high occurrences of childhood trauma, indicating that nurture plays a critical role in both lifestyles.

Obesity And Childhood Trauma

Obviously, not everyone battling obesity has a history of childhood abuse. The association between childhood obesity and sexual abuse is strongest in children and adults with *severe* obesity.[33] Binge Eating Disorder (BED) is three to four times more common in obese people who report a history of childhood sexual abuse.[34] The simple explanation for this is that compulsive eating is one of the ways the abuse victim manages the depression brought on by the effects of sexual abuse, i.e., poor self-esteem, poor body image, drug abuse, and impulsive behavior. One survey found that 55% of obesity patients acknowledged some form of childhood sexual abuse[35] (that is even higher than the homosexual research).[32] Another analysis of 57,000 women found that those who experienced childhood physical or sexual abuse were twice as likely to be addicted to food than those who did not.[36]

For those who have suffered the horrors of childhood abuse, please hear me: food can never heal a broken heart. God wants to be the fortress you run to in time of need. He wants to be your comforter, your defense, and your strength. If you have been the victim of childhood abuse, whether verbal, physical, or sexual, your help begins by allowing Jesus Christ to heal your splintered soul.

Therapists help victims of childhood abuse by getting them to talk about it. If you have been abused and have never sought out professional help in overcoming the abuse of your past, I highly encourage you to do

---

See also http://www.voiceofthevoiceless.info/lesbian-feminist-camille-paglia-sexual-orientation-is-fluid-and-can-change.

James Tillman, "Study: Homosexuality Linked with Childhood Trauma," July 27, 2013, https://www.lifesitenews.com/news/study-homosexuality-linked-with-childhood-trauma.

[33] http://www.obesityaction.org/community/article-library/sexual-abuse-and-obesity-whats-the-link/

[34] Ibid.

[35] https://www.theatlantic.com/health/archive/2015/12/sexual-abuse-victims-obesity/420186/

[36] Ibid.

so.[37] Please don't allow the pain of your past to cut your life short. God has great things for you.

What To Do Now

The purpose of this chapter is not to put forth a new diet or training regimen. My aim has been to present the doctrine of self-control in order to ignite your faith to the point of bearing the fruit of self-control with your food appetites. No matter what the next fad diet will be, it will only be successful when mixed with self-control. No matter what the next fitness sensation will be, it will only be beneficial if it is mixed with self-control.

I recommend praying self-control scriptures at every meal and before every workout. We have not because we ask not. Self-control is like every other Bible promise, we must ask for it in prayer in order to possess it. I am not talking about sheer willpower. The world aims for that without God's help. I am talking about asking God, through the power of the Holy Spirit, to endow us with a supernatural ability to restrain our flesh. We are speaking of the ninth supernatural fruit of the Holy Spirit—self-control. We must ask for it in prayer. It is our Father's good pleasure to help us bear this fruit for His glory. Self-control glorifies God. Self-control can help you beat fat!

- Is God dealing with you about your weight?
- Do you live to eat or eat to live?
- Do you overeat? Is it for comfort or out of boredom?
- What changes will you make going forward?

Minister's Moment

As a minister of the Gospel, you must be a living example of righteous doctrine. This includes self-control. Your personal body and your food appetites must be disciplined. God's people watch you. They observe you. Many will make decisions based on how you live and what you permit in your own life. It is time to face the truth: it can be very difficult for people

---

[37] I also highly recommend the book *The Wounded Heart: Hope For Adult Victims of Childhood Sexual Abuse* by Dr. Dan B. Allender.

to receive from a fat preacher. A minister is held to a much higher standard than laity. We are to show the people the Gospel is not just preachable—it is livable! I will conclude with haunting words from the Apostle Paul:

> **But I discipline my body and make it my slave, so that, after I have preached to others, I myself will not be disqualified.** **1 Corinthians 9:27 (NASB)**

> **That each of you knows how to control his own body in holiness and honor,** **1 Thessalonians 4:4 (CSB)**

CHAPTER 8
FINAL THOUGHTS

This has been a book about the doctrine of self-control. What are we to do? We obey the Bible. We honor God. We present our bodies a living sacrifice unto Him. We keep our flesh under. That is what we are commanded to do. But self-control goes far beyond fat, broke, and crazy. Self-control is an aid for every area of life. Every appetite of life can quickly dissolve into a life-controlling addiction.

Salvation and the new birth were afforded to us that we might walk in a freedom unknown to mankind since the Garden of Eden. No longer bound to sin or its appetites, we are free and alive unto God. Titus 2:1-2 teaches us that the grace of God that brings salvation has appeared to all men, teaching us to deny ungodliness and worldly lusts and to live self-controlled. For a Christian to live bound to a sensual appetite is to squander God's grace. Have you received the grace of God in vain?

Self-control must be applied to anything we are in bondage to. This includes social media, entertainment, sports, video games, alcohol, cigarettes, sleep, gambling, and pornography. What can you not walk away from? What can't you quit? Self-control can help you beat that addiction. Western Christians often forget that flesh is meant to suffer, not be pampered. We crucify our flesh. We put to death the deeds of our flesh, and the Bible calls this freedom. Indulgence leads to death. Crucifixion leads to life.

I have been a runner since I was a teenager. Some years ago I was out running my route. It was a very hot summer day and the run was beginning to take its toll on me. I had a habit of always greeting or waving to the people of whatever neighborhood I was running through. On this particular day I saw a lady sitting on her front porch smoking a cigarette, so I waved at her and yelled, "How's it going?" To which she playfully replied, "Well ... I'm not as hot or miserable as you are right now. But, then again, I'm not in shape like you." "Very true," I answered. This brief exchange has stuck with me for years. That lady recognized that in that moment I was miserable and she was comfortable, but in the long run I would be the one comfortable and she would be miserable.

In 1972, Fram Oil Filters ran a series of commercials where a mechanic held up an oil filter and said, "You can pay me now," and then holding up an engine piston said, "or you can pay me later." It was a play on the old adage: an ounce of prevention is worth a pound of cure. The wisdom of the marketing strategy was brilliant: you can pay a little for an oil filter now, or you can pay a whole lot more for an engine overhaul later. Either way, you are going to pay something. Self-control is God's way of helping us pay cheaply for things now so that we don't suffer tremendously later. May you find freedom and victory through the fruit of self-control!

Acknowledgements

Special thanks to the editing team, Eva Dingwall and Kiley Baldwin for the countless revisions, editing sessions, and last-minute mark-ups. Thank you to Darrell Kerley for the graphic design and cover layout. I also wish to thank Bobbie Scudder, Emma Scudder, Patti Newman, Tiffany Andrews, Susan Keith, Wanda Dingwall, Danielle Girt, and Sarah Dingwall for their proofreading and feedback. Thank you to Hannah Keith for the time spent on formatting (it's a hated job, but someone has to do it). Thank you also to Dr. Kevin Baird, Pastor Chace Gordon, and Pastor Cary Gordon for their doctrinal critique and feedback. I am especially grateful for my wife, Manda, for keeping things going as I finished up this "book writing season."